SALAD SAMPLER

from
Quilting in the Country

This book is presented by
Jane Quinn
Quilting in the Country
Bozeman, Montana

Cover artwork by Liz Silliman
Three Forks, Montana

Edited by Anne Quinn Egan and Julie Bush Maletic
~ a big job!

Many thanks to Bill Quinn for his computer skills
but mostly for his good humor and patience.

Graphic Design and Layout by Media Works,
Bozeman, Montana

Photos taken by Linda Best and the many friends
of Quilting in the Country,
Bozeman, Montana

Recipes submitted by all the wonderful folks who have
taken the time to be a part of Quilting in the Country.
This cookbook would not have been complete without your recipes.
Thank you.

When our daughter Anne was born, I never imagined she would be
assisting me as editor of Quilting in the Country's Salad Sampler cookbook
and become my best friend. During this endeavor, I was honored to observe
Anne's talent in the "fixing up" process of this book.

She inscribed a cookbook she had given me this way,
"We both share a love for cookbooks and cooking and this book fits both.
I know you'll enjoy it ~ I will too! Many happy experiences."

Thank you special daughter!

I grew up on a farm in Iowa, and as you can probably guess, the garden was a huge part of my life, not to mention my diet! In fact, one of my earliest memories as a young child is of the beautiful bright green loose-leaf lettuce available only from our garden and a staple long before loose-leaf lettuce became all the rage! My mother would coat the leaves with a dressing made of heavy cream from our neighbor's milk cow.

Salads also bring me back to Exira's most popular holiday - Independence Day. Of all the holidays, this is the one I miss most from my childhood days. My mother always put me to work weeding the garden to earn extra money for a new outfit and admission to the carnival rides at our community celebration in town. Mom would draw a line with a stick to show how much I would earn if I did a really good job weeding that patch of garden. Usually she would award a quarter with each section, small increments to keep my interest up, I think! When I reflect on this time in my life, the memories come flooding back: decorating the 4-H float for the parade, and marching in the 100+ degree weather in a wool band uniform (how did we survive?).

I have to admit, however, that the most impressive part of the entire holiday was after the parade when all my distant relatives - and those not so distant - gathered at my grandmother's house for a huge potluck. There was a large array of salads, but mostly cabbage, potato, and macaroni. Remember the days before pasta became a part of our vocabulary? My father preferred my mother's potato salad and he could always identify it by the familiar clear-ridged glass bowl. Saran Wrap® had not been invented yet, so we had plenty of flies! Of course, this celebration would not have been complete without baked beans, fried chicken - very fresh, I might add, since a young chicken had recently been butchered - cherry pies, from first-of-the-season cherries off our trees, rhubarb-mulberry pie, and homemade ice cream. Escalloped corn was also a popular part of the Iowa menu. And we always had Jell-O salads - all kinds and colors!

This brings me to why I decided to create my second cookbook. I was inspired by my family's tradition of serving Ribbon Salad with oyster stew on Christmas Eve. I believe the original Ribbon Salad was shared by my Aunt Fern and I don't remember a Christmas Eve without it in probably 50 years! I have added another salad to my contemporary version of this meal - mostly green with fresh vegetables. My Aunt Louise's recipe for Pimento Salad also appears in this cookbook since it is what I remember being served faithfully at all Thanksgiving dinners, along with goose, turkey, escalloped oysters and all the other yummy trimmings.

Many of us have recipe collections. Oh, I'm sure we don't think of them as collections, but they truly are. I have a friend who solicits recipes from her friends, but only if they are in the recognizable handwriting of that friend. My recipe box is full of such recipes and I enjoy finding a spattered favorite in my mother's very characteristic handwriting. Some of the recipes are like having a visit from a dear old friend.

When I asked for contributions to this book, many salad makers had forgotten about the salads they used to make. Those great oldies had been pushed to the back of the recipe box in favor of the popular salads of the day. Thankfully some oldies are included here along with many fresh new variations. I hope you enjoy the book as much as I enjoyed putting it together and I hope it brings your memories flooding back. Like quilts, recipes bind the generations together. The recipes here are truly a collection - A Salad Sampler.

CHICKEN
SALADS

Winter has a way of working itself into your bones, your brain, your soul. Stay inside. Unfurl your favorite quilt. Use it as a shawl or total cover for protection from the season. Prepare a cup of tea. Grab the cat! Kindle a fire and read a good quilt book or magazine and dream of quilts.

I have so many quilts spinning around in my head, don't you? We're all affected by the world around us. This fall Bill and I were blessed to have the opportunity to visit Paris, Venice, Florence and Rome. While most tourists were clicking photos of famous buildings, statues and art, I was snapping pictures of architectural elements, especially floors. For color and texture inspiration, I brought home some stones, shells and worn bottle glass from the seaside.

While in Italy, we learned that our former exchange student son will be married next June and that calls for a quilt composed of photos taken on the trip and some graphic interpretations of the photographed details. Also in June, our son Paul will be graduating with an MBA from American University and I have long promised him a t-shirt quilt made from the shirts he collected while a student in Hong Kong. This one is envisioned with the world pieced in the center showing his travels from Montana to China. And, there must be quilts for our second grandchild expected at the end of May!

There is never a lack of reasons for the gift of a quilt - baby's first Christmas, first day of school, homecoming, prom, over-the-hill birthdays, anniversaries, or vacations. Whatever calls for creating something with special meaning - something personal.

Stitch by stitch, piece by piece we add to our quilts. In our dearest dreams we don't imagine that our quilts will be honored by a future generation but quilts are a wonderful legacy. Yesterday, in the mail, I received two thank you notes for quilts I had given as gifts - one for a new baby's nursery with clouds and star motifs, the other from my Godchild given as a high school graduation gift. Now I'm not expecting these quilts to become heirlooms but I did feel proud knowing they were received with such appreciation and who knows, maybe they will pass from generation to generation.

Our lives are built on memories and times shared with people we love. Memories and love shared across generations touches our heart, delights our eyes and leaves us with a smile. For years, special times and quilts have gone hand in hand, because no matter what the occasion, quilts are appreciated. Giving a quilt can be as personal and loving as your feelings. All your quilts and stories are important to us at Quilting in the Country. It is listening to you that helps us shape the pages of our business.

Thank you very much.

Jane

P.S. Many of you have inquired concerning Wacky, the orphaned baby raccoon, we adopted this summer. Wacky left us early last fall and then returned about six weeks later for a big bowl of cat food and to let us know she was still alive. We haven't seen her since, but maybe next spring she will return to show us some of her own offspring. She was a delight!

Oriental Chicken Salad

Maryanne Harbour
Bozeman, Montana

Maryanne says she loves to collect recipes and this one came from a picnic.

Salad:

2   whole cooked chicken breasts, chilled and cubed

1/4   cup slivered almonds, lightly toasted

1/4   cup sesame seeds, lightly toasted

1   medium head cabbage, finely chopped

2   green onions with tops, thinly sliced

2   packages oriental-flavor ramen type noodles, uncooked and broken into small pieces (flavoring packets reserved)

Dressing:

1/3   cup lemon juice

1   cup oil

1/2   cup seasoned rice vinegar

2   seasoning packets from the oriental ramen noodles

Make dressing 24 hours ahead of time. When ready to serve, combine all salad ingredients in a large bowl and toss with dressing.

Hot Chicken Salad

Jane Quinn
Bozeman, Montana

I have many fond memories of my quilt mentor and friend, Jane Edie. Of course she was a great quilter, but she also loved cooking, entertaining, and serving food in creative and inventive ways. It is special to find her handwritten recipes among the others in my recipe file.

1	stewing hen, 3 1/2-pounds or larger
1	cup celery, chopped
1	cup slivered almonds
2	tablespoons onion, minced
1	10 1/2-ounce can cream of chicken soup
1	cup mayonnaise
2	tablespoons lemon juice
3/4	teaspoon salt
1/4	teaspoon pepper
	buttered bread crumbs or crushed potato chips
	paprika

Steam or stew chicken until tender. Remove bones, and skin from meat and cut into bite size pieces. Mix with all ingredients, except crumbs and paprika. Turn into a two-quart casserole dish. Top with crumbs or chips, and paprika. Bake in a 350 degree oven, uncovered , for about 30-40 minutes, or until bubbly. (Salad can be frozen before or after baking.)

Serves 6-8

Colorado Cobb Salad

Malinda Ringo
Denver, Colorado

Salad:

1/2	head Boston Bibb lettuce
1/2	bunch watercress
1/2	head Romaine lettuce
3	medium tomatoes, diced
3	half chicken breasts, cooked and diced
6	strips crisp bacon, crumbled
1	ripe avocado, diced
2	hard-boiled eggs, chopped
1/3	cup bleu cheese, crumbled
	salt and pepper

Vinaigrette Dressing:

3/4	cup salad oil
1/4	cup red wine vinegar
1/2	teaspoon salt
1/4	teaspoon pepper
2	teaspoons Dijon mustard

Shred lettuce and place in a large salad bowl. Arrange remaining ingredients in strips across the salad. Toss with dressing, salt, and pepper before serving.

Serves 4

Fruited Chicken Salad

Gary and Diane Arganbright, "The Quilting Hen and Antiques"
Carter, Montana

I was recently treated to an outing at this special shop outside Great Falls,
Montana. Hospitality abounds!

4	cups cooked chicken, diced
1	15-ounce can pineapple chunks, drained
1	cup celery, chopped
1	11-ounce can mandarin oranges, drained
1/2	cup ripe olives, sliced
1/2	cup green peppers, chopped
2	tablespoons onion, grated
1	cup mayonnaise or salad dressing
1	tablespoon prepared mustard
1	15-ounce can chow mein noodles

In a large bowl, combine chicken, pineapple, celery, oranges, olives, green pepper, and onion. Blend salad dressing and mustard. Toss gently with chicken mixture. Cover and chill several hours or overnight. Just before serving, mix with chow mein noodles and turn into a lettuce-lined serving bowl.

Makes 8 servings

On The Go Salad

Heidi Furst
Butte, Montana

Heidi is our sales rep from Aptex and since she's a quilter herself, she has lots of good ideas on using the products. Heidi's salad is so good you'd never expect it to be this easy!

1	head iceberg lettuce, broken
2	deli chicken breasts (Heidi uses *KFC Original*), broken into small pieces - skin and all
1 1/2	cups red grapes, cut in half
	mayonnaise
	salt and pepper

Toss all ingredients with enough mayonnaise to "dress" the salad. Season to your taste. Serve with a good quality French bread.

Santa Fe Chicken Salad

Pat Binger, "All In Stitches"
Polson, Montana

3/4	cup grilled chicken breasts, diced
4	cups lettuce
1/2	cup bleu cheese
1/2	cup cilantro, chopped
1/2	cup spicy peanuts
	ranch dressing mixed with bar-b-que sauce to taste

Mix all ingredients and serve with tortilla chips or popovers. Adjust ingredients to seasoning you prefer.

Serves 4

Chicken Macadamia Salad

Bunny Haines
Missoula, Montana

3 cups cooked chicken or turkey, cubed

1 can water chestnuts, sliced

3/4 cup celery, sliced

1 cup macadamia nuts, chopped, or toasted slivered almonds, divided

1 cup pineapple chunks, drained

1/2 pound seedless grapes

1 cup mayonnaise

1/4 teaspoon curry powder

1 1/2 teaspoons soy sauce

paprika, to taste

pineapple chunks and grape clusters (for garnish)

Place chicken, water chestnuts, celery, and 3/4 cup nuts in a large bowl; mix together lightly but thoroughly. Add pineapple chunks and grapes, mixing lightly. Mix together mayonnaise, curry, and soy sauce. Toss mayonnaise mixture with chicken mixture. Refrigerate covered until chilled. Sprinkle top of salad with remaining 1/4 cup nuts and paprika. Garnish with additional pineapple chunks and grape clusters, or mandarin oranges.

Serves 6

Oriental Chicken Salad

Laura Heine
Billings, Montana

Laura is an internationally-known quilter. In addition to owning the quilt shop, Fiber Works, in Billings, she is a thread artist for YLI thread and designer of our Salad Sampler challenge fabric by King's Road.

Salad:

10	ounces grilled or breaded chicken breast (Laura uses chicken tenders already cooked at the deli)
1/2	head green cabbage, shredded
1/4	head red cabbage, shredded
1/2	pound carrots, shredded
1/2	head iceberg or Romaine lettuce, shredded
1/2	cup green onions, sliced
	sliced almonds
	oriental noodles

Dressing:

3/4	cup honey
5	tablespoons mayonnaise
1/2	teaspoon sesame oil
1/3	cup white vinegar
4	teaspoons Grey Poupon Dijon mustard

Use an electric beater to mix the dressing ingredients. Chill. Combine salad ingredients and top with toasted sliced almonds, oriental noodles, and dressing.

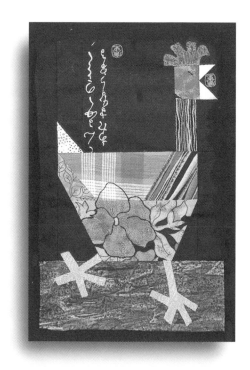

Mainliner Chicken Salad

Pat Walter
Pine Island, Minnesota

For this recipe, Pat closely replicated the Mainliner Chicken Salad she always enjoys at Red Lobster. She likes to serve this special salad with cheddar cheese biscuits prepared from a recipe a friend gave her - they sort of "clone" the biscuits served with this salad at Red Lobster.

4	cups lettuce
	croutons
	tomatoes, sliced
	zucchini slices, grilled
	onion, cut into rings
	chicken breast, grilled and sliced

Tear lettuce into a low-rimmed salad/soup bowl. Garnish with croutons, tomatoes, zucchini slices, onion rings, and top with the grilled chicken breast. Serve this salad with your favorite honey-mustard dressing on the side.

Cheddar Cheese Biscuits

Pat Walker
Pine Island, Minnesota

1/4	cup butter, melted
	crushed garlic, to taste
2	cups *Bisquick* baking mix
2/3	cup milk
1	tablespoon chives, dried
1/2	cup cheddar cheese shredded

Preheat oven to 450 degrees. Melt butter with garlic. Set aside and keep warm. Mix baking mix, milk, chives, and cheese until a soft dough forms. Beat vigorously for 30 seconds. Drop dough by spoonfuls on an ungreased baking sheet. Bake 8-10 minutes, or until biscuits are golden brown. Remove from oven. Brush immediately with garlic butter mixture before removing from baking sheet.

Chicken Salad

Jean Naismith Gullicks
Grand Forks, North Dakota

Jean is a member of a multi-generation quilting family. Grandmother, aunts, and family friends are quilting and cheering the kids on!

3	cups cooked chicken, diced
1	tablespoon minced onion
3	tablespoons lemon juice
1	cup grapes
1	cup celery, diced
1/3	cup slivered almonds
1	cup *Miracle Whip* salad dressing
1	teaspoon salt
1	cup pineapple tidbits
1	cup mandarin oranges
2	cups cooked macaroni rings
1	cup cream, whipped
	lettuce leaves

Toss chicken and onion in lemon juice. Mix all remaining ingredients, except lettuce and chill. Serve in lettuce cups.

Celebrate life.

Keep it simple.

Laugh out loud.

Cherish friendships.

Say it like it is.

Make people smile. — Fresh Ink

Potpourri Chicken Salad

Debbie Bennett
Bozeman, Montana

We all love Debbie's perky attitude and the new pattern ideas she comes up with inspire us all!

3   cups cooked chicken, chopped

3   stalks celery, finely chopped

1/2   cup onion, finely chopped

1/2   cup water chestnuts, finely chopped

1/2   cup black olives, finely chopped

1/2   cup shelled sunflower seeds

1   cup (approximately) mayonnaise

1   tablespoon *Grey Poupon* mustard

salt and pepper to taste

dash of cayenne pepper

Mix the first six ingredients in a large bowl. These proportions are approximate - adjust to suit your taste. Add the mayonnaise and mustard. Again, adjust to your liking. Last, add the spices.

Spread the salad on a flour tortilla and roll it up, or serve on a bed of lettuce with mandarin oranges on the side.

Jade Chicken Salad with Peanut Dressing

Susan Howard
Helena, Montana

Susan and her mother, Lois Irish, are enthusiastic clients at Quilting in the Country. Lois submitted this delicious-sounding recipe for Susan.

Salad:

6   boneless, skinless chicken breast halves (about 3-pounds)

1   3-ounce package ramen noodles, crumbled (discard seasoning package)

1   head (about 8 cups) Romaine lettuce, cut into bite-size pieces

1/2 head (about 4 cups) napa cabbage, cut into bite-size pieces

6   green onions (about 3/4 cup), sliced

1   8-ounce can water chestnuts, drained and coarsely chopped

1   small cucumber (about 1 1/2 cups), chopped into 1/2-inch pieces

4   plum tomatoes, chopped into 1/2-inch pieces

    napa cabbage leaves for serving

Peanut Dressing:

1 1/2 tablespoons fresh ginger, finely minced

3/4 cup soy sauce

6   tablespoons sugar

6   tablespoons distilled white vinegar

9   tablespoons vegetable oil

1/4 cup chunky peanut butter

Instructions continued on the next page.

To make dressing, combine all ingredients in a glass jar or medium-size bowl and shake or mix until blended.

To make salad, cut all fat from chicken and place breasts in a large plastic zipper bag. Add 1/2 cup peanut dressing. Marinate chicken in the refrigerator for 4 to 6 hours, turning once. Meanwhile, crumble noodles and bake in oven at 350 degrees until golden, about 10 minutes. Prepare lettuce and cabbage, wrap in paper towels and put in a plastic bag, and refrigerate. Remove chicken from marinade and blot dry with paper towels. Grill over hot coals or broil in a shallow roasting pan lined with heavy foil, 3 to 4 inches from flame, for 3-6 minutes per side, or until browned and cooked through.

To assemble, slice chicken into thin strips. In a large bowl, combine chicken, lettuce, cabbage, green onions, water chestnuts, cucumber, and tomatoes. Refrigerate until ready to serve. Line salad plates or a platter with napa cabbage leaves. Add as much dressing to salad as needed and toss well. Spoon salad onto cabbage leaves and sprinkle with noodles.

8 to 10 main dish servings

Chicken Salad

From the unknown quilter - sorry!

2	cups mayonnaise
1/4	cup (or 1/2 small jar) yellow mustard
1/2	cup onion, grated
4	cups (2 whole breasts) cooked chicken, diced
1	cup mandarin oranges, drained
1	cup pineapple tidbits, drained
1	cup celery, diced
1/2	cup stuffed green olives, sliced
1	cup cashews, optional
1	large can chow mein noodles

Combine all ingredients, except chow mein noodles, and chill overnight. Just before serving, add chow mein noodles.

Serves approximately 12

Chicken Salad Veronica

Gwen Marshall
Australia

This is an updated version of the old Waldorf salad, with chicken added. The salad is best made when seedless grapes are in season; it is distinguished by delicious, curry-flavored mayonnaise.

4	whole chicken breasts, or 8 half breasts
2	teaspoons curry powder
2	tablespoons chicken stock
1	egg yolk
2	teaspoons Dijon mustard
2	tablespoons lemon juice
1 1/2	cups salad oil
	dash cayenne pepper
	dash Worcestershire sauce
3/4	cup chopped pecans, walnuts, or blanched almonds
4	sticks tender celery, sliced
2	cups seedless white grapes, stems removed
2	tart apples, peeled and thinly sliced
	lettuce leaves to serve
	parsley sprigs or small bunches of grapes (to garnish)
	salt
	freshly ground white pepper

Cover chicken breasts with lightly salted water, bring to a simmer, and poach for 8 minutes, or until cooked through. Cool in the stock, then remove skin and bones and cut flesh into neat, bite-size pieces. Reserve 2 tablespoons of the stock for this dish (the rest can be refrigerated for other uses).

Combine curry powder and the 2 tablespoons of stock in a small saucepan. Bring to a boil, stirring, then put aside to cool. Place egg yolk in a bowl and beat in mustard, lemon juice, and salt and pepper to taste. Gradually beat in the oil - drop by drop - using a wire whisk. When the mixture begins to thicken, add oil in a thin, steady stream, and continue beating until mayonnaise is thick. Beat in the curry mixture and season with cayenne pepper and Worcestershire sauce to taste.

Place chicken pieces, nuts, celery, grapes, and apples in a bowl and combine. Add curry mayonnaise and fold together. Arrange a bed of lettuce leaves on a pretty serving dish, spoon salad on top, and garnish with parsley sprigs or a small bunches of grapes.

Salad Superb

Gwen Marshall
Australia

When you want to impress a luncheon guest, serve this sumptuous salad. It is expensive, but worth it!

1/2	ripe avocado, peeled and cut into wedges
	squeeze of fresh lemon juice
1/2	firm lettuce head
4	cooked asparagus spears, cut into short lengths
1/2	chicken breast, cooked and cut into chunks
4	ounces cooked prawns, peeled
	salt
	freshly ground white pepper
2	ounces sliced smoked salmon
2	ounces black caviar, or lumpfish roe
1/4	cup mayonnaise
2	tablespoons sour cream
	celery leaves to garnish

Squeeze a little lemon juice over the avocado. Make a bed of lettuce leaves on a serving plate, and arrange avocado, asparagus, chicken, and prawns over it. Season with salt and pepper. Arrange salmon slices overlapping on top, forming a cup-shape, and spoon caviar into the middle. Combine mayonnaise and sour cream. Spoon some over the salad, and serve remainder separately. Garnish salad with celery leaves.

Serves 2

Chicken Waldorf Salad

Eleanor Christian
Bozeman, Montana

Eleanor's great grandparents homesteaded our place. Her support and enthusiasm for what we've done has always pleased us immensely.

4-5	cooked chicken breasts, diced
1	cup whole walnuts, toasted
1	8-ounce package snow peas (blanche 1 minute, then cool)
1	cup mayonnaise
3	tablespoons Dijon mustard
3	tablespoons white wine vinegar
1	teaspoon coarse salt
1/2	teaspoon white pepper
2	small tart green apples, chopped
5	celery stalks, chopped
	salt
	pepper

Toss all ingredients and refrigerate.

Chicken Curry Salad

Mary Ellen Woolley
Bozeman, Montana

Mary Ellen submitted this recipe for her sister-in-law, Mary Lou.

2	pounds chicken breasts
1/2	cup water
1	onion, sliced
	celery top
1	teaspoon salt
3 or 4	peppercorns, or 1/2 teaspoon pepper
2/3	cup water
2/3	cup precooked rice (such as *Minute Rice*)
1/4	teaspoon salt
1	cup mayonnaise
1	tablespoon lemon juice
1/2	teaspoon curry powder
1	teaspoon onion, grated
1	teaspoon salt
1/8	teaspoon pepper
1	cup celery, diced
1	13 1/2-ounce can pineapple tidbits, drained
1/2	cup coconut, flaked

Simmer chicken with 1/2 cup of water, onion, celery, salt, and peppercorns for 30 minutes until tender. Cool. Remove meat from bones (if you use chicken with bones) and dice.

Bring 2/3 cup of water to boiling. Stir in rice, cover, and remove from heat. Let stand 5 minutes. Uncover and cool.

Mix mayonnaise, lemon juice, curry powder, grated onion, salt, and pepper. Combine celery, pineapple, and coconut with chicken, rice, and dressing. Toss lightly and chill.

Sweet and Savory Chicken Salad

Lorna Wharrier
Great Britain

This is another wonderful addition to the cookbook from my English friend, Lorna.

Salad:

2   cups cooked chicken, cut into chunks

1   20-ounce can unsweetened pineapple chunks, drained

1   10-ounce can unsweetened mandarin oranges, drained

1   small cucumber, diced

1   scallion, finely chopped

Dressing:

1/2 cup plain low-fat yogurt

1   tablespoon lemon juice

3/4 teaspoon dried tarragon

Mix dressing ingredients together. Mix all salad ingredients in a bowl. Pour the dressing over the salad and toss lightly. Serve with a green salad of your choice.

The more you know- the more you care for things.

Chicken Salad in Cantaloupe Halves

Jo Ireland
Bozeman, Montana

This is a tasty and different chicken salad! Really refreshing!

1   small yellow bell pepper
    (about 6-ounces)

1   medium papaya
    (about 1-pound)

3   cups cooked
    chicken, shredded

1/4 cup fresh cilantro leaves
    or parsley, minced

2   teaspoons lime
    peel, grated

1/4 cup lime juice

1/4 cup orange juice

2   cantaloupes (about 2-
    pounds each), cut into
    halves and seeded

    salt

    pepper

Stem, seed, and finely chop the bell pepper. Cut the papaya into halves, discard seeds, remove skin with a knife, and cut into 1/2 inch cubes.

Combine bell pepper, papaya, chicken, and cilantro. If making ahead, cover and chill up to 4 hours. Stir together lime peel, lime juice, and orange juice. Pour over chicken mixture; stir to mix. Spoon into melon halves.

4 servings

Indian Chicken Salad with Chutney

Kathy Center
Bozeman, Montana

Kathy helps us in so many ways at Quilting in the Country. She is clever and talented in such different ways that it continues to amaze me.

Salad:

1	tablespoon lemon juice
2	teaspoons curry powder
	salt and pepper, to taste
2	whole skinless boneless chicken breasts
1	head Romaine lettuce, shredded
2	large tomatoes, diced
1/2	cup green onion, sliced
1	cup cheddar cheese, grated
2	cups sweetened coconut, toasted
1	cup slivered almonds, toasted
1	cup black olives, sliced
1 1/2	cups apple pear chutney
2	cups crispy chow mein noodles

Honey Mustard Dressing:

1/3	cup whole grain mustard
1/2	cup honey
1	teaspoon cayenne pepper
1/2	cup vegetable oil
1/2	cup red wine vinegar

Combine lemon juice, curry powder, salt, and pepper. Marinate chicken breasts in lemon juice combination for 1 hour. Grill or broil chicken until done, cool, and dice. Layer next 3 ingredients, and top with diced chicken. After chicken, layer with next 4 ingredients. Chill. When ready to serve, arrange a nice ring of chutney on top of salad and add noodles. Serve making sure everyone gets a portion of all ingredients. Pass the dressing to serve on top.

For dressing, combine ingredients in a container with a tight-fitting lid. Warm slightly and shake well to serve.

Molded Chicken Salad

Pat Binger - "All In Stitches"
Polson, Montana

1	package unflavored gelatin
1/4	cup cold chicken broth
1/2	cup hot chicken broth
1/4	teaspoon salt
1	tablespoon lemon juice
3/4	cup mayonnaise
1	cup cooked chicken, diced
3	tablespoons green pepper, minced
3/4	cup celery, finely chopped
	salad greens
	pimentos (optional)

Soak gelatin in cold chicken broth. Dissolve in hot chicken broth. Add salt and cool. Add lemon juice and mayonnaise. Stir in cooled chicken, green pepper, and celery. Turn into oiled bread pan and chill. Unmold on bed of salad greens and garnish with pimentos.

Big Event Chicken Salad

Barb Dena
Parachute, Colorado

Salad:

8	cups (2 quarts) cooked chicken, cubed
2	cups water chestnuts, sliced
3	cups pineapple chunks
2	cups grapes
2	cups celery, diced
2	cups dates, diced
2	cups nuts, coarsely chopped, or sunflower or sesame seeds

Dressing:

2 1/2	cups real mayonnaise
1/2	cup chicken broth
1	teaspoon (or to taste) curry powder
2	teaspoons soy sauce
	leafy lettuce

Combine salad ingredients in a large bowl. Combine dressing in a separate bowl and add to chicken salad mixture just enough to moisten. Blend carefully.

Chicken Salad

Jane Quinn
Bozeman, Montana

Salad:

1   small chicken, or 2-
2 1/2-pounds chicken
breast, boiled (or fried)
and chopped into
small pieces

1   medium head lettuce

4   green onions

1/4 slivered almonds

2   tablespoons
sesame seeds

2-3 ounces rice sticks

Dressing:

1   teaspoon salt

1/2 teaspoon pepper

2   tablespoons white
vinegar

1   teaspoon monosodium
(optional)

1/4 cup salad oil

Shred lettuce, chop onions, add almonds, and sesame seeds. Fry rice sticks and cool. Just before serving, add chicken and rice sticks. Toss and add dressing.

Serves 8

Chinese Chicken Salad

Marianne Liebmann
Bozeman, Montana

This salad is very fast and easy, but delicious. Marianne uses vegetables she has on hand. She sometimes substitutes cooked roast beef for the chicken. It is a great way to use up leftovers. Despite being a very busy mom, wife, generous community member, and owner of Langohr's Greenhouse, Marianne makes time to produce some great quilts!

Salad:

1	bag pre-washed mixed lettuce
1	bag pre-washed vegetables (broccoli, cauliflower, carrots, and celery)
1	whole cooked boneless chicken breast, diced
2	tablespoons sesame seed

Dressing:

1	teaspoon fresh ginger, minced
1	teaspoon fresh garlic, minced
1/4	cup rice vinegar
1/4	cup soy sauce
2	tablespoons sugar
1	tablespoon hoisin sauce
1 1/2	teaspoon Dijon mustard
1 1/2	teaspoons dark sesame oil
1/2	cup olive oil

Process dressing ingredients in a blender or food processor for 30-45 seconds.

Divide lettuce among 4 plates, chop vegetables into bite-size pieces, and add to plates. Divide chicken and add to plates. Drizzle dressing on salad and sprinkle with sesame seeds.

"Saying nothing sometimes says the most."
— Celestial Seasonings

Chicken Romaine Salad with Raspberry Dressing

Mary Jo Nuss
Bismarck, North Dakota

I tried Mary Jo's recipe at a salad luncheon/birthday celebration for a friend. It's a great one!

Salad:

1	pound package Romaine hearts, torn into bite-size pieces
4	green onions, thinly sliced
1	pint strawberries, quartered
1/4	cup toasted slivered almonds
4	grilled or broiled chicken breast halves, sliced

Dressing:

3/4	cup sugar
3/4	cup vegetable oil
1/2	cup raspberry vinegar
1/2	teaspoon grated onion
2	drops Worcestershire sauce
1/2	teaspoon celery seed
1	pinch dry mustard
5	tablespoons salad dressing

Whisk dressing ingredients together until well blended and chill. Toast almonds in microwave 3-4 minutes, let cool. Divide greens among 4 plates. Top each with a sliced chicken breast. Drizzle with dressing. Serve with garlic toast.

4 servings.

Luncheon Turkey Salad

Jan Rutledge
Bozeman, Montana

Salad:

2 1/2	pounds turkey, cooked and diced
1	20-ounce can sliced water chestnuts, well drained
2	pounds seedless grapes, halved
2	cups celery, sliced
1	20-ounce can pineapple chunks, well drained
1-2	cups sliced almonds, toasted

Dressing:

3	cups mayonnaise
1/2	tablespoon curry powder (use 1 tablespoon if preferred)
2	tablespoons soy sauce
2	tablespoons lemon juice

Mix dressing and salad ingredients together the night before serving.

Chicken Salad

Barb Cribb
Bozeman, Montana

This is great served as a sandwich filling or scooped onto a bed of lettuce with tomato wedges. Barb recommends using chicken left over from dinner the night before. Besides being a talented quiltmaker, designer, and teacher, Barb is a wonderful cook.

1	large whole baked chicken
1/3	cup celery, finely chopped
2	tablespoons sweet pickle relish
	seasoned salt to taste
	mayonnaise

Prepare chicken by picking the meat off the bones and chopping it very fine, or use a food processor. Mix all ingredients together, adding enough mayonnaise for a good spreading consistency.

Crunchy Chicken Salad

Sue Anne Iman, "In Good Company"
Hamilton, Montana

Sue Anne and 3 other women own a pattern company. We love their annual trunk show at Quilting in the Country's outdoor quilt show.

2	cups boned chicken, chopped, or tuna or shrimp
1 1/2	cups carrots, shredded
1	cup celery, chopped
1	tablespoon onion, grated
1	cup mayonnaise, thin with cream or milk if desired
2	small cans chow mein noodles

Mix all ingredients except noodles. Add noodles before serving.

Chicken Curry Salad

Sharon Andriolo
Bozeman, Montana

I tried Sharon's salad with leftover barbecued chicken - it was fabulous!

Salad:

3	cups cooked chicken, chopped
1 3/4	cups seedless red grapes, halved
1	11-ounce can mandarin orange slices, drained
1	8-ounce can sliced water chestnuts, drained
1	cup celery, sliced
	leaf lettuce

Dressing:

1	8-ounce carton plain yogurt
2	teaspoons soy sauce
2	teaspoons lemon juice
3/4	teaspoon curry powder

Combine dressing ingredients and mix well. Combine chicken, grapes, oranges, water chestnuts, and celery.

Toss lightly with dressing. Chill up to 8 hours. Spoon salad on lettuce-lined plates.

6-8 servings

Honey Mustard Salad

Jane Quinn
Bozeman, Montana

Salad:

1 1/2 pounds cooked chicken breast, cooled, boned, and skinned

1 1/2 cups celery, chopped into 1/2-inch pieces

2 tablespoons yellow onion, minced

Dressing:

1/2 cup honey mustard

3/4 cup mayonnaise

4 teaspoons celery seed

1/2 teaspoon garlic powder

1/2 teaspoon coarse black pepper

1/2 teaspoon salt

Hand tear chicken into bite-size chunks; put into a bowl. Add celery and onion; toss. For dressing, stir together mustard, mayonnaise, celery seed, garlic powder, pepper, and salt. Fold the dressing into chicken and vegetable mixture.

Serves 6-8

Chicken Curry Fruit Salad

Cara Schaer
Billings, Montana

Cara and I met in the church nursery when we first moved to Bozeman over 30 years ago. We've been like family ever since. What better than to have a dear friend who loves to cook and eat!

Salad:

- 3 whole chicken breasts, cooked, skinned and cut into bite size pieces (shred chicken if you prefer a smoother texture)
- 3/4 cup green or red seedless grapes, sliced
- 1 cup celery, sliced
- 1/2 cup golden raisins
- 1/2 cup combination of pitted, dried prunes and fresh purple plums, diced (use 3/4 cup if preferred)
- 1 cup fresh chives, minced
- 1 cup roasted macadamia nuts

  salt and pepper to taste

  red leaf lettuce

Dressing:

- 1 1/2 cups mayonnaise
- 1/2 teaspoon curry powder (use 3/4 cup if preferred)
- 1 teaspoon dried tarragon
- 1 tablespoon honey

  salt and pepper to taste

Mix all dressing ingredients with a whisk until well blended. Chill. (The dressing is also delicious as a spread with turkey, ham, or warm pork sandwiches.)

Combine all salad ingredients except the nuts and toss with dressing. Chill for 2-3 hours for spices to enhance the salad mixture. Mix the nuts in just before serving. Serve salad on a bed of red leaf lettuce. (This same mixture may be served in pita bread as a sandwich by spreading some of the dressing on the inside of halved pita bread. Line the pita pocket with lettuce leaves and fill with chicken salad.)

CRANBERRY
SALADS

ANYWAY

People are unreasonable, illogical, and self-centered,
LOVE THEM ANYWAY

If you do good, people will accuse you of selfish ulterior motives,
DO GOOD ANYWAY

If you are successful, you will win false and true enemies,
SUCCEED ANYWAY

The good you do will be forgotten tomorrow,
DO GOOD ANYWAY

Honesty and frankness make you vulnerable,
BE HONEST AND FRANK ANYWAY

What you spent years building may be destroyed overnight,
BUILD ANYWAY

People really need help but may attack you if you help them,
HELP PEOPLE ANYWAY

Give the world the best you have and you'll get kicked in the teeth,
GIVE THE WORLD THE BEST YOU'VE GOT ANYWAY

— From a sign on the wall of Shishu Bhavan, the Children's House in Calcutta

Dorothy's Cranberry Salad

Juli Rognlie
Bozeman, Montana

Juli remembers this salad from her mother as a Thanksgiving dinner tradition.
Juli's mom, Dorothy, was the nurse at our pediatrician's office when my children
were growing up.

2	cups raw cranberries, chopped
2	cups small marshmallows
1	large orange, sectioned and diced
1	cup sugar
2	cups apple, diced
3/4	cup green grapes, sliced in half
3/4	cup walnuts, chopped
1	cup cream, whipped

Mix cranberries, marshmallows, orange, and sugar and chill overnight. Stir in the apple, grapes, walnuts, and whipped cream; serve chilled.

Jan's Cranberry Salad

Brenda R. Hauer - "All In Stitches"
Polson, Montana

This Big Sky quilt shop has recently changed ownership and we hear it's a
darling shop.

2	cups raw cranberries
1	orange
2	cups granulated sugar
1	cup nutmeats
1	cup celery, diced
1	large package lemon gelatin

Grind cranberries and orange (including peel) in food grinder.

Add sugar and set aside.

Make gelatin with 3-1/2 cups hot water. Chill until syrupy. Add cranberry/orange mixture, nutmeats, and celery. Mold.

Cranberry Jello Salad

Kay Gannon and Bunny Franklin, "Scraps & Threads Quilt Guild"
Eureka, Montana

*Susan Gilman sent this recipe from a group of ladies that help to maintain her
sanity by escaping from her shop, "Glacier Quilts", in Columbia Falls,
Montana, one a day a month. Susan says she does, however, inevitably end up
answering quilting questions!*

2   3-ounce packages
    raspberry gelatin

2   cups boiling water

1   can whole
    cranberry sauce

1   pint good quality
    sour cream

    chopped nuts (optional)

Mix together gelatin and water;
let partially set. Add cranberry
sauce. Fold in sour cream and
nuts. Pour into a 9 x 13 inch
cake pan and chill.

Cranberry-Pineapple Salad

Marian Neill
Whitehall, Montana

2   packages lemon gelatin

1 3/4 cups boiling water

1   can whole
    cranberry sauce

8   ounces *7-Up* soda

1   medium can crushed
    pineapple, undrained

1   8-ounce package
    cream cheese

1   envelope *Dream
    Whip* topping

    toasted pecans

Mix gelatin with water; stir in
cranberry sauce and cool. Add
7-Up and pineapple. Pour into a
9 x 13 inch pan and let set.
Beat cream cheese; add
prepared topping, and mix.
Spread on gelatin. Sprinkle with
toasted pecans.

Cranberry Chicken Salad

Kimberli Hart McCullough
Big Timber, Montana

Kimberli is a self-professed "salad-a-holic" who believes a refreshing salad is perfect for our Montana afternoons, or a quilt retreat. Kimberli makes a difference in the lives of her students in Big Timber. She introduces them to the "lifetime sport" of quilting!

1   3-ounce package strawberry gelatin

1   cup boiling water

1   16-ounce can jellied cranberry sauce

3   cups cooked chicken, cubed

1   cup celery, diagonally sliced

1   2-ounce jar pimiento, drained and chopped

1   tablespoon lemon juice

1/4   teaspoon lemon rind

3/4   cup mayonnaise
      salt and pepper to taste
      lettuce leaves

Dissolve gelatin in water. In a saucepan, soften cranberry sauce over low heat. Add to gelatin mixture. Stir well. Pour into a greased 3-cup ring mold. Chill until firm, about 4 hours.

In a large bowl, combine chicken, celery, pimento, lemon juice, lemon rind, and mayonnaise. Gently mix together. Refrigerate until gelatin is set. Before serving, add salt and pepper to the chicken mixture. Unmold gelatin onto lettuce leaves. Put the chicken mixture in the center of the mold. Serve immediately. (For added color and zest, slice an orange, give the slices a slight twist, and lay them on the edge of the serving platter.)

I would not exchange the laughter of my heart
for all the fortunes of the multitudes. Kahil Gibran

Cranberry-Cheese Mold

Janice Ardans
Davis, California

Janice is a wonderful friend and hostess. She even managed to prepare amazing meals when she had five little girls at home!

1	3-ounce package orange-pineapple gelatin
1	cup boiling water
1	cup orange juice
1	3-ounce package cream cheese, softened
1/2	cup cream, whipped
1/4	cup pecans, chopped
1	envelope unflavored gelatin
1/4	cup cold water
1	1-pound can whole cranberry sauce
2	tablespoons lemon juice
1/4	teaspoon allspice
1/8	teaspoon nutmeg
1	cup orange sections
1	7-ounce (1 cup) bottle ginger ale

Dissolve gelatin in boiling water. Stir in orange juice, chill until partially set. Blend cream cheese into whipped cream. Add pecans; fold into gelatin mixture. Pour into a 9 X 9 X 2 inch dish, chill until almost firm. Soften unflavored gelatin in cold water; dissolve over hot water. Combine remaining ingredients; stir in softened gelatin. Pour over cream cheese layer. Chill 4-5 hours. Cut into squares to serve.

9 servings

Cranberry Salad

Cydell Chambers
Bozeman, Montana

A longtime interior designer and quilter, Cydell and I have known each other for many years. Unfortunately for us she will be moving to Idaho to be near family.

2	cups cranberries
1 1/2	cups water
1	cup sugar
1	6-ounce package cherry gelatin
1	15-ounce can crushed pineapple with juice
1	Granny Smith apple, peeled and chopped
1	cup pecans, chopped

Simmer cranberries in water for 10 minutes. Add the sugar and stir well. Then add the gelatin and stir. When these ingredients are partially cooked, add the pineapple, apple, and pecans. Pour into a 2 quart mold and chill until set.

Jane's Cranberry Salad

Jane Dobbie
Bozeman, Montana

2	bags fresh cranberries, ground or chopped
	sugar
1	pint whipping cream
	vanilla
	powdered sugar
	walnuts, chopped
1	cup red seedless grapes, cut in half

Combine cranberries with an equal amount of sugar. Drain in the refrigerator overnight. Whip cream with vanilla and powdered sugar. Add nuts, grapes, and cranberries.

Cranberry Ice

Diane Donnelly
Bozeman, Montana

This is a delightful addition to holiday meals as an appetizer or dessert. It would probably taste good in the summer, too, if you could get the cranberries. Diane found this recipe while going through an old box of kitchen stuff; the recipe was in her mother's handwriting. Since her mother passed away in 1975, Diane took special notice of it and tried it for Thanksgiving. She says it was delicious and made her feel that her mother was there celebrating with the family. Like quilts, family recipes connect the generations.

1 quart fresh cranberries	Cook cranberries in the hot water.
2 3/4 cups hot water	Run through sieve. Add sugar and
2 cups sugar	lemon juice. Let mixture come to
4 tablespoons lemon juice	a boil. Dissolve gelatin in 1 cup
1 tablespoon gelatin	cold water, add to boiling mixture, and freeze. Serve.

Dreams are the touchstones of our characters.
Henry David Thoreau

Cranberry/Orange Salad

Kathy Conger
Bozeman, Montana

This salad is great for Thanksgiving, but also a cool option in the summer.

4 cups raw cranberries, washed with stems and pink berries removed	Blend small amounts of cranberries and sugar in a blender until fairly course
3 oranges, peeled	consistency. Add oranges and
1 cup (or more if desired) sugar	blend. Serve in orange peel shells or a serving bowl.

Peggy's Cranberry Salad

Peggy Lipsey
Bozeman, Montana

Peggy is a former employee and a good friend of Quilting in the Country.

1	small box cherry gelatin
1	cup boiling water
1	pound can whole cranberry sauce
1	medium can mandarin oranges, drained
1	medium can crushed pineapple, drained
1/2	cup walnuts, chopped
	bananas or grapes (optional)

Pour boiling water over gelatin and mix well. Add cranberry sauce and mix. Fold in remaining fruit and mix well. Chill until set.

Cranberry Salad

Eva Veltkamp
Bozeman, Montana

Eva's cranberry salad is very tasty with turkey and great for holiday dinners.

2	packages orange gelatin
2	cups hot water
3/4	cups sugar
2	cups cranberry juice
1/2	lemon, juice only
1	pound cranberries, ground
1	orange, ground
	celery, chopped (optional)
	pecans, optional
	Miracle Whip dressing

Dissolve gelatin in hot water, add sugar, and stir. Add cranberry juice and lemon juice. Refrigerate gelatin while grinding cranberries and orange. Add to gelatin mixture along with celery and pecans. Refrigerate. Serve with *Miracle Whip* dressing.

Cranberry Mold

Lois Wambolt
Bozeman, Montana

Lois got this recipe when she student-taught and has been making it ever since. She says it keeps very well and is liked by everyone, even those who don't particularly like cranberries. Lois likes the flavor pecans bring to this festive salad.

1   6-ounce package raspberry gelatin

1   teaspoon salt

2   cups hot water

1   cup cold water

4   teaspoons lemon juice

2   cups whole cranberry sauce

1   cup canned crushed pineapple, drained

1   cup celery, diced

1   cup apple, diced

1/2 cup nuts, pecans or others

Dissolve gelatin and salt in hot water. Add cold water and lemon juice. Chill until slightly thickened. Fold in cranberry sauce, pineapple, celery, nuts, and apple. Pour into mold or a 9 x 13 inch pan. Chill until firm.

DRESSINGS

Winter, isn't it the greatest time for quilters? Now don't get me wrong. I enjoy winter outdoor activities, in fact, I was a ski bum during an earlier period in my life. But while many Northerners are flying south for the winter months or are seriously pouring over glitzy travel brochures, I have my own recipe for relaxation during the winter's deep freeze. I don't feel a need to hop on the next plane to escape the blahs. I plan to stay put and enjoy the happy secret of dormancy. Somewhere along the way we were conditioned to think of winter as a time of depressed psychological state. Dormancy, a necessary condition of plant life, is important in our lives too. In a way, we freeze and thaw too. Plants require a rest. Maybe we require a necessary nap too, a little being out of season. We accept that in our perennials. Why don't we just say it's okay if we aren't always blooming?

We think we _have_ to be productive _all_ the time. Maybe being fallow and resting is just what could be thought of as creative waiting. Maybe the next stage of our winter is doing absolutely nothing and when you've had enough of that, clear your mind with a good day of skiing or even a little snow shoveling. Under this blanket of snow, I'm sure we will know just how to make the best of the winter.

My Grandma Bauer only made quilts in the winter. She was occupied with gardening, preserving, and canning during the summer months. During the spring planting and fall harvest, there were always hired hands to feed. Come winter, Grandma was ready to meet with the other farm women in the neighborhood. They got together to quilt in a group, simply called Club. Quiltmaking played a social role and satisfied their need to be thrifty and industrious during hard times. Strong bonds were created among these rural women. The Club was a way for them to find companionship and friends and exchange patterns, fabric (feed sacks, lots of times) and ideas. Grandmother could give of herself, while forgetting her troubles. I'm sure that Grandma didn't think of herself as being involved with an American tradition. For her it was an expression of love. She certainly didn't think she was creating heirlooms that would be passed down for generations to come.

When my grandparents downsized from their large frame farm house to a small bungalow in town, Grandma was not prepared to get rid of her quilts. A special part of visiting Grandmother overnight was selecting the linens to make up your own bed. The closet in the spare bedroom was stacked from floor to ceiling with quilts. There were wonderful embroidered and crocheted pillowcases too. The quilt I usually chose to use on my bed was the Album quilt made by all the ladies from The Club.

The schedule contains a class, Emma's Friendship Quilt, which is my version of a tribute to my grandma. My aunts cleared Grandma's house after her death and I asked about the quilt. No one seemed to know where it was, but I do have other quilts from grandma.

So while Grandma's beautiful flower beds were lying dormant in the wintertime, she was making quilts and was undoubtedly influenced not only by the tactile experience, but also the visual experience of colors from her garden. The color combinations were endless in her quilts just as they were in her summer garden. But she, like I, did not want to be too long removed from anything that involved fabric, needles and thread.

My grandmother did not leave any scrapbooks and I probably won't either, but I think maybe she knew what I have known for sometime. Quilting touches the emotions and provides time to contemplate the ebbs and flows of life. While quilting you have a lot of time to think through problems and plan for the future. Life can be contemplated while quilting. Quilts are my scrapbook. They tell a story, provide a link to the past, and record a family history.

Take a long winter's nap, then prepare to make a quilt, the time of creative waiting is over ...

Jane

Spinach Salad Dressing

Robin Stilwell, "Quilt-essentials"
Butte, Montana

2 1/2 tablespoons red
      wine vinegar

2   tablespoons sour cream

3/4 teaspoon salt

1/4 teaspoon dry mustard

1   tablespoon sugar

1   tablespoon parsley,
      chopped

1   clove garlic, crushed

1/2 cup oil

      black pepper,
      coarsely ground

Place all ingredients except oil in a food processor and mix until smooth. With processor running, gradually add oil and process until smooth. Serve over a salad of spinach, boiled eggs, sliced red onion, and crumbled bacon.

Caesar Salad Dressing

Marianne Liebmann
Bozeman, Montana

Marianne also likes to add bite-size pieces of leftover meat to this salad.

3   cloves garlic,
      finely chopped

3/4 cup mayonnaise

1/4 teaspoon anchovy paste,
      or to taste

1/3 cup parmesan
      cheese, grated

1   tablespoon lemon juice

1   teaspoon Worcestershire
      sauce

1   teaspoon Dijon mustard

Blend all ingredients well. Toss dressing with one 16-ounce bag chopped Romaine lettuce. Mix well. Serve with additional grated parmesan cheese and croutons of your choice.

Dressing for Fruit Salad

Marian Neill
Whitehall, Montana

This dressing freezes well and helps keep fruit fresh.

1 cup pineapple juice
3 tablespoons cornstarch
1/2 cup sugar
1/4 cup lemon juice
1/4 cup orange juice
1 tablespoon lime juice, (optional)

Cook pineapple juice, cornstarch, and sugar until smooth and thick. Add lemon juice, orange juice, and lime juice.

Fruit Salad Dressing

Marian Neill
Whitehall, Montana

1 7-ounce jar marshmallow cream
1 8-ounce package cream cheese
1 tablespoon orange rind, grated
 dash ginger

Mix all ingredients well. Serve with fruit salad.

Poppy Seed Dressing for Fruit

Robin Stilwell, "Quilt-essentials"
Butte, Montana

1/3	cup cider vinegar
3/4	cup sugar
1 1/2	tablespoons onion juice, or finely minced onion
1	teaspoon dry mustard
1/2	teaspoon salt
1	cup oil
1 1/2	tablespoons poppy seeds

Place first 5 ingredients in a food processor and pulse 2 or 3 times. Gradually add oil while processor is running. Add poppy seeds and pulse 2 or 3 times. Serve over a fruit salad of melons, strawberries, bananas, kiwi, etc.

She was one of those happily creative beings who pleases without effort, makes friends everywhere, and takes life so gracefully and easily that less fortunate souls are tempted to believe that such are born under a lucky star.
Louisa May Alcott

Salad Dressing

Barb Dena
Parachute, Colorado

1	dry packet *Hidden Valley Ranch* Dressing
1	small jar real mayonnaise
1	small carton small-curd cottage cheese

Run all ingredients through a blender until smooth, or mix by hand to make a wonderful dip!

Cole Slaw Dressing

Marianne Liebmann
Bozeman, Montana

Marianne and her husband own Langohr's Greenhouse in Bozeman.
Marianne always includes recipes in their newsletter and I always try them!

1   cup mayonnaise
2   tablespoons white vinegar
1/4 cup sugar
1   tablespoon sour cream
1/2 teaspoon horseradish
1/8 teaspoon paprika
1   16-ounce bag coleslaw

Combine mayonnaise, vinegar, sugar, sour cream, horseradish, and paprika. Toss with coleslaw.

Merry Berry Fruit Salad Dressing

Joyce Slingsby
Bozeman, Montana

Joyce is an inspiration! We want to be just like her when we grow up! This
salad can also be served as a dessert in a small compote with whipped cream.

1   cup plain yogurt
1   cup fresh or frozen berries of choice
1/4 teaspoon ground cinnamon
1-2 drops vanilla extract

Blend all ingredients in a blender until berries are pureed. Chill well before serving.

Honey Salad Dressing

Jane Quinn
Bozeman, Montana

3/4 cup sugar
1 teaspoon paprika
1 tablespoon lemon juice
1/3 cup honey
1 teaspoon onion, grated
1 teaspoon celery salt
5 tablespoons vinegar
1 teaspoon mustard
1/4 teaspoon salt
1 cup salad oil

Mix all ingredients thoroughly.

If we take care of the moments, the years will take care of themselves.
Maria Edgeworth

Dressing for Spinach Salad

Patti's Bernina
Sunburst, Montana

1 small onion, chopped
1/2 cup ketchup
1/2 cup vinegar
1/2 cup vegetable oil
3/4 cup sugar
1 tablespoon Worcestershire sauce
2 teaspoons salt

Put all ingredients in a jar and shake well.

Bleu Cheese Dressing

Lynda Faulkner
Helena, Montana

1	clove garlic
1/2	sweet onion
2	inch piece green pepper
1	quart *Best Food* mayonnaise
4	ounce package bleu cheese
1	tablespoon lemon juice
1/2	teaspoon Worcestershire sauce

Chop garlic, onion, and green pepper in food processor; add mayonnaise. Stir in bleu cheese, lemon juice, and Worcestershire sauce. Flavor improves after aging 3-4 days in refrigerator.

Katherine's Salad Dressing

Katherine Atteberry
Bozeman, Montana

Katherine has been a good friend for many years. We share a mutual love of cooking!

1/2	cup salad oil
1/3	cup red wine vinegar
1	clove garlic, minced
2	tablespoons brown sugar
2	tablespoons chives
1	tablespoon curry
1	teaspoon soy sauce

Blend all ingredients. Toss with salad greens, 1 can mandarin oranges, and a cup of grapes; sprinkle with toasted almonds, and decorate with ripe avocados.

Rice Wine Dressing

Pat Paynich
Bozeman, Montana

1	tablespoon light olive oil
1/2	cup rice vinegar
1	teaspoon sugar
1/2	teaspoon salt

Dissolve sugar and salt in rice vinegar. Add olive oil. Mix together; serve over salad.

French Dressing

Jane Quinn
Bozeman, Montana

This dressing has been a standby in our house for many years.

1	cup salad oil
1/3	cup ketchup
1/2	cup sugar
1	teaspoon salt
1/4	cup vinegar
1	teaspoon instant onion

Blend well.

Makes 1 pint

Pear-Nectar Vinaigrette

Corrine Hoffart
Bozeman, Montana

1/3	cup white wine vinegar
1/3	cup salad oil
1/3	cup pear nectar
1	teaspoon Dijon mustard
1/4	teaspoon salt
1/8	teaspoon pepper

In a screw-top jar combine all ingredients. Cover and shake well to mix. Store in the refrigerator for up to 1 week. Shake before serving.

Makes about 1 cup

Colony Club Salad Dressing

Juli Rognlie
Bozeman, Montana

This recipe is from Matt Rognlie's (Juli's husband) grandmother. It is wonderful for any green salad.

1/2 cup sugar

1/2 cup vinegar (cider vinegar or rice vinegar)

1 teaspoon dry mustard

3/4 cup vegetable oil

1 can tomato soup

2 teaspoons Worcestershire sauce

1 medium onion, chopped

1 green pepper, chopped

1 clove garlic, minced

Blend all ingredients in a blender.

Fresh Garden Relish

Marge Sande, "Quilt-A-Way"
Great Falls, Montana

1	cup carrots, finely sliced
1/2	cup green pepper, chopped
1/2	cup celery, chopped
1/4	cup green onion, chopped
3	tablespoons apple cider vinegar
2	tablespoons honey
1/2	teaspoon dill weed, or more to taste

Combine all ingredients and let stand in refrigerator until used.

Growing old is mandatory,
but growing up is optional.

Ginger Salad Dressing

Lynda Faulkner
Helena, Montana

1/2	cup salad oil
1/4	cup soy sauce
1/3	cup onion, diced
1/4	cup celery, diced
3	tablespoons plus 1 teaspoon rice vinegar
2	tablespoons fresh ginger root, peeled
2	teaspoons sugar
1/2	teaspoon ketchup
1/4	teaspoon black pepper

Combine all ingredients in a food processor and process until vegetables are pureed.

FRUIT SALADS

A recent study has indicated that quilt fabric gives off certain Pheromones that actually hypnotize women and cause them to purchase ungodly amounts of the substance!

When stored in large quantities in enclosed spaces, these Pheromones cause memory loss and induce the nesting syndrome (similar to the one squirrels have before the onset of winter, i.e. storing food), therefore perpetuating that species, and preventing a population loss due to their kind being cut up into pieces and mixed with others. Sound tests have also revealed that these fabrics emit very high-pitched sounds, heard only by a select few breed of women known as "quilters."

When played backwards on a record, the sounds are heard as chants "buy me, cut me, sew me!" In order to overcome the so-called "feeding frenzy effect" that these fabrics cause, face masks and ear plugs must be worn when entering a storage facility to avoid being pulled into their grip. Studies also point to an indication that aliens have inhabited the earth, helping to spread the effect that these fabrics have on the human population. They are called fabric store clerks.

It's also common for these same Pheromones to cause a pathological need to secret fabric purchases away when taken home (or at least to blend them into the existing stash). When asked by a significant other if the fabric is new, the reply is "I've had it for awhile!" From the newsletter of the Quilt Guild of Greater Houston

Curried Fruit and Vegetable Salad

Phyllis Egan
Butte, Montana

Phyllis is my daughter's mother-in-law.

Salad:

- lettuce, any kind or mixture, even spinach
- mandarin oranges, drained
- grapes, halved
- almonds, sliced
- avocado

Dressing:

- 1/2 cup salad oil
- 1/3 cup vinegar
- 1   clove garlic, minced
- 2   tablespoons brown sugar
- 1   tablespoon curry powder
- 1   teaspoon soy sauce

Mix dressing ingredients in a blender. Toss with salad ingredients and serve.

We turn, not older with years, but newer every day.
Emily Dickinson

Quilting Bee Salad

Pam Wills
Curwensville, Pennsylvania

- 1   20-ounce can crushed pineapple, drained
- 1/2 cup lemon juice
- 1   can *Eagle Brand* milk
- 1   large carton *Cool Whip* topping
- 1/2 cup nuts, chopped (optional)

Mix all ingredients, except nuts, together and spread in a 11 X 13 inch glass baking dish. Sprinkle with nuts. Refrigerate.

Summer Fruit and Bacon Salad

Jane Quinn
Bozeman, Montana

Salad:

1	large (or two medium) ripe melons, chilled
8	fresh plums, halved, or 16 whole, pitted prunes
1	basket strawberries, sliced
4	large oranges, peeled and sectioned
16	bacon slices, cooked until crisp
	Romaine lettuce leaves

Ginger-Orange Nut Dressing:

1	cup mayonnaise or unflavored yogurt
1/4	cup orange juice
1	tablespoon orange peel, grated
1	tablespoon sugar
1	teaspoon fresh ginger, minced
1/2	cup toasted almonds, chopped

Mix all dressing ingredients. This may be prepared up to two days before serving.

Cut melon into thin wedges. Line plates or platter with lettuce leaves. Arrange fruits and bacon on top. Pass dressing.

8 servings

*Some people say trying
is all that matters
but unfortunately
it's only the first step;
sometimes you have
to win one too.
Miracle on the 17th Green*

Summer Melon Salad

Beth Kovich
Seattle, Washington

Beth is employed at "That Patchwork Place." It has become a wonderful tradition that Beth teaches at Quilting in the Country every summer when she and her husband vacation in Ennis, Montana. Beth commented that this salad is a very refreshing combination! She feels that it is worth it to make melon balls rather than chunks.

1	large honeydew melon, cut into chunks or balls
1	large cantaloupe, cut into chunks or balls
1/2	seedless watermelon, cut into chunks or balls
10	mint leaves, cut into tiny strips
1/4	cup sugar
1/4	cup water
1/2	teaspoon ginger, freshly grated (use 1 teaspoon if preferred)
	juice of 1 lime
	zest of 1 lime

Combine sugar, water, lime juice, zest and ginger. Use as a dressing for the fruit.

Funeral Salad

Jan Wallace
Whitehall, Montana

For a number of years, a group of quilters met in a group called
Country Living. We shared many wonderful potlucks. Jan introduced
us to this delicious dish so named because it was contributed to the funeral
dinner many times.

1	large carton *Cool Whip* topping
2	8-ounce cartons strawberry yogurt
1	package frozen strawberries

Mix together and serve in a pretty bowl. Yum!

Fresh Fruit Cups

Shirley Kraus
Paul, Idaho

Shirley has won many awards for her outstanding quilts. As for her salad,
any seasonal fruit works well for this frosty delight!

1/2	cup sugar
1 1/2	cups water
1	6-ounce can frozen lemonade
1	6-ounce can frozen orange juice
1	can crushed pineapple
1	small box strawberries
1	small jar cherries
3	large bananas
	seedless grapes, to taste

Dissolve sugar in water, add frozen lemonade, frozen orange juice, and crushed pineapple; mix well. Add strawberries, cherries, bananas, and grapes; again mix well. Put fruit mixture in cups and freeze. Approximately 30 to 45 minutes before serving, remove cups from freezer, let melt, and serve icy. The cups will be the consistency of slush.

Delight Salad

Dorothy Kern
Bozeman, Montana

1   cup buttermilk
1   small box instant
    vanilla pudding
1   8-ounce package
    whipped topping
1   cup mandarin
    oranges, drained
1   can crushed
    pineapple, drained
1 1/2 rows chocolate striped
    cookies, crumbled

Mix buttermilk and dry pudding
until thick. Fold in whipped
topping and drained fruit, mixing
well. Just before serving, stir in
crumbled cookies.

Fruit Salad

Theresa Schweitzer
Bozeman, Montana

*We love the treats Theresa brings us - especially Almond Roca, but you can
count on this salad being delicious, too.*

1   cup buttermilk
1   package instant French
    vanilla pudding
1   12-ounce carton
    extra-creamy
    Cool Whip topping
3   cups grapes
1   quart strawberries
3   large bananas

Beat buttermilk and dry pudding
together; fold in *Cool Whip*. Cut
grapes and strawberries, and add
to above mixture. Shortly before
serving, add cut bananas.

Serves 12

Pearl Tapioca Salad

Marilyn Hanson
Bozeman, Montana

This recipe also doubles as a tasty dessert. Marilyn Hanson submitted it on behalf of her late aunt, Jeanette Hastings Hamilton of Kenton, Ohio. Marilyn's aunt always fixed this salad when her family was visiting Ohio relatives. It takes preparation time, but is "oh-so-good". This is a very special salad for a very special occasion. Interestingly enough, the original recipe calls for a 49 cent package of walnuts, my how times have changed!

1   package pearl tapioca
    pinch of salt
1   large can crushed
    pineapple, drained
3/4 cup sugar
1/2 teaspoon vanilla
1   package black or
    English walnuts
1/2 pint whipped cream

Soak tapioca and salt for 24 hours in warm water to cover. After soaking, cook tapioca over low-medium heat for 30 minutes or more. When cooked clear, add pineapple, sugar, and vanilla. Chill overnight. Add walnut pieces and whipped cream.

Pretzel Fluff Salad

Jean Paulsen
Exira, Iowa

Jean is a loyal high school friend from Iowa.

1	cup pretzels, crushed
1/3	cup sugar
1/2	cup margarine, melted
1	8-ounce package cream cheese
1/2	cup sugar
1	8-ounce container *Cool Whip* topping
1	20-ounce can pineapple tidbits, drained

Mix together pretzels, 1/3 cup sugar, and melted margarine. Spread mixture in a 9 x 13 inch pan. Bake at 400 degrees for 7 minutes. Stir to break up; cool. Cream the cream cheese with 1/2 cup sugar. Fold in the *Cool Whip* and pineapple. Chill 2 or 3 hours. When ready to serve, fold the pretzel mixture into the salad.

Joy's Fruit Salad

Jane Quinn
Bozeman, Montana

The important ingredient here is the Wilderness Pie Filling.

1	can peach or apricot *Wilderness Pie Filling*
1	package frozen strawberries or raspberries
	canned fruit cocktail
	marshmallows
	grapes
	pineapple
	bananas
	anything else that turns you on

Pour pie filling into a large bowl and combine remaining ingredients, making sure to add bananas at the end.

Fruit Poached In Wine

Joyce Slingsby
Bozeman, Montana

Joyce's mother used to make this for her bridge club. While she prepared it, Joyce and her sister could have a "little" - long before they were old enough to drink it! The sauce is good with anything.

2	cups red or white wine
3/4	cup sugar
1/2	fresh lemon, peel and slice
2	tablespoons lemon juice
1	cinnamon stick
4	large pieces fresh fruit of choice (pear, peach, nectarine, orange, apple), peeled and cored

Place first 5 ingredients in a saucepan over medium heat until sugar is dissolved and mixture comes to a boil. Stir. Reduce heat and simmer 5 minutes. Add fruit and simmer until fruit is tender. Do not boil! Let fruit sit in juice for 20 minutes before serving. Serve on a lettuce leaf, top with juice or fruit dressing.

5-Cup Salad

Kathy Conger
Bozeman, Montana

Kathy's quick and easy recipe is great for brunch. The recipe is very, very easy and also very, very good! When Kathy was a little girl it was her favorite and she thought it must be very hard to make because her mother only made it for holidays!

1	cup mini-marshmallows
1	cup crushed pineapple, drained
1	cup mandarin oranges, drained
1	cup coconut
1/2	cup sour cream

Mix all ingredients and chill.

Frozen Fruit Salad

Sharon Davis
Bozeman, Montana, and Dallas, Texas

Sharon told me that she served this favorite recipe at a bridal shower for her daughter's friend.

1   3-ounce package
    cream cheese
2   tablespoons lemon juice
1/3 cup mayonnaise
2   tablespoons sugar
1   cup crushed
    pineapple, drained
1   cup mandarin
    oranges, drained
1/2 cup maraschino
    cherries, chopped
1/2 cup pecans, chopped
1   cup *Cool Whip* topping

Combine cream cheese, lemon juice, mayonnaise, and sugar until well blended. (A mixer or food processor works well.) Add fruit and pecans to cream cheese mixture. Fold in *Cool Whip*. Freeze in 2 12-ounce orange juice cans. To serve, run cans under warm water, push out salad, and slice.

Tropical Fruit Salad

Barb Dena
Parachute, Colorado

Barb tells me she's not sure if it is the fruit or the tequila that she likes about this salad!

Salad:

1	bunch seedless grapes, halved
3	cups fresh pineapple, cut into chunks
2	pints fresh strawberries, halved
2	grapefruit, sectioned
2	navel oranges, sectioned
2	ripe mangoes, peeled and cut into chunks
1	teaspoon lime peel, grated
4	kiwi fruit, peeled and cut into chunks (peel by running a spoon along the inside of skin)

Syrup:

3/4	cup sugar
1/4	cup water
1/4	cup lime juice, fresh or bottled
2-3	tablespoons tequila

For syrup, bring sugar and water to boil. Reduce heat. Simmer 2 minutes until sugar is dissolved completely. Remove from heat. Stir in lime juice and tequila. Cool to room temperature. Refrigerate 2 hours.

For salad, combine all fruits. Toss gently. Just before serving; stir lime peel into syrup and drizzle syrup over salad.

Snicker-Apple Salad

Kimberli Hart McCullough
Big Timber, Montana

My friend, Kimberli, uses 5-6 Snickers bars in this recipe, saying one can never get enough chocolate! I certainly agree!

3-4 Snickers bars, frozen

1 12-ounce carton
Cool Whip topping

4-5 green apples,
unpeeled and diced

Unwrap candy bars and place them in a clean cloth. Break bars into small to medium pieces with a hammer. Mix candy, *Cool Whip*, and diced apples. Serve.

Hints: Place apples in a lemon juice and water mixture to avoid browning. Place the candy bar in a zip-lock bag and use a rolling pin to break it up.

Pimento Frozen Salad

Louise Bauer
Exira, Iowa

Louise was married to my father's brother, George Bauer. She is a very energetic soul who brought great fun to our family gatherings in my hometown of Exira. At one time, she owned a drive-in root beer stand. I was a carhop, not on roller-skates.

2 jars pimento cheese

1/2 cup mayonnaise

40 marshmallows, cut
into pieces

1/2 cup nuts, chopped

1 large can crushed
pineapple, undrained

1 pint cream, whipped

Cream cheese and mayonnaise; add marshmallows, nuts, and pineapple. Fold in whipped cream. This recipe will fill a large baking dish and keeps in the freezer for a month.

Frozen Cheese Salad

Janet H. Ganson
Billings, Montana

This is Janet's family favorite for holidays and anytime a special salad is needed!

1   3-ounce package
    cream cheese

1   20-ounce can crushed
    pineapple, drained

18 marshmallows, cut into
    small pieces

    chopped walnuts,
    to taste

1   small bottle maraschino
    cherries, finely chopped

1/2 pint whipping cream

2   tablespoons salad
    dressing

Mash cream cheese and blend with the pineapple. Add marshmallows, chopped walnuts, and cherries. Whip cream and add salad dressing. Fold into fruit. Place in a refrigerator dish 3-4 hours, or overnight. This salad lasts several days in the refrigerator.

Grand Marnier Fresh Fruit Cup

Jan Rutledge
Bozeman, Montana

1/4 cup *Grand
    Marnier* liqueur

1/4 cup sugar

2   pints blueberries

1/2 pound Bing cherries,
    halved and pitted

4   pounds peaches, peeled
    and sliced

1   pint fresh raspberries

    yogurt (optional)

Mix *Grand Marnier* and sugar, stirring to dissolve sugar. Prepare fruits and gently mix together. Add liqueur mixture to fruit. Refrigerate until ready to serve. Serve in individual cups, with yogurt spooned over top.

Frog Eye Salad

Sue Broyles
Rapelje, Montana

This salad is a Broyles' family favorite. It makes a huge amount, so it works well for potlucks, graduation parties, wedding celebrations, and anywhere else you need to feed many people.

1	cup sugar
2	tablespoons flour
1/2	teaspoon salt
1 3/4	cup pineapple juice
2	eggs, beaten
1	tablespoon lemon juice
3	quarts water
2	teaspoons salt
1	tablespoon cooking oil
1	16-ounce package *Acini de Pepe* pasta
2	20-ounce cans pineapple tidbits, drained
2	20-ounce cans crushed pineapple, drained
1	20-ounce can fruit cocktail, drained
1	8-ounce carton *Cool Whip* topping
1	cup miniature marshmallows (optional)
1	cup coconut (optional)
3	11-ounce cans mandarin oranges

Combine sugar, flour, and 1/2 teaspoon salt. Gradually stir in pineapple juice and eggs. Cook mixture over moderate heat, stirring until thickened. Add lemon juice. Cool mixture to room temperature.

Bring water, 2 teaspoons salt, and oil to a boil. Add pasta. Cook at a rolling boil until the pasta is done. Drain pasta, rinse with cold water, drain again, and cool to room temperature.

Combine egg mixture and pasta. Mix lightly, but thoroughly. Refrigerate overnight in an airtight container. Add remaining ingredients, and mix lightly. Be sure to add mandarin oranges last so they hold their shape. Refrigerate until chilled in an airtight container. Salad may be refrigerated for as long as a week.

30 servings

Ambrosia Waldorf

Barb Dena
Parachute, Colorado

1	cup whipping cream
3/4	cup mandarin oranges, drained
2	bananas, sliced
1/2	cup seedless green grapes, halved
1/3	cup coconut
2	cups apple, diced
1	cup celery, diced
1/2	cup walnut pieces
3	tablespoons lemon juice
1	cup real mayonnaise
1	tablespoon sugar
	small handful mini marshmallows

Beat whipping cream with mixer until fluffy, gradually adding sugar. Combine fruit, celery and nuts; sprinkle with lemon juice. Fold whipped cream into mayonnaise, add fruit and marshmallows. Chill.

What would you attempt to do if you knew you could not fail?

Cookie Salad

Deb Wilson and Susan Gilman, "Glacier Quilts"
Columbia Falls, Montana

Susan submitted this salad saying it is just too good not to share!

1	5-ounce package vanilla instant pudding
1	cup milk
1	16-ounce container *Cool Whip* topping
2	small cans mandarin oranges, drained
1	package fudge striped cookies, crushed

Mix together pudding and milk; add *Cool Whip*. Stir in oranges and cookies. Garnish with a few cookie pieces.

GRAIN SALADS

$\mathcal{W}$elcome $\mathcal{D}$ear $\mathcal{F}$riends,

All right, I'll admit it. I've been procrastinating. Big Time! On my calendar several days were blocked out for the purpose of writing this newsletter, as it's important to have a refuge from this busy place. I needed a nook to sit down in, a private place. I needed a self-imposed time-out, a meditative moment. Sometimes what seems so insignificant in passing can be a valuable idea if you just have time to let it unfold and be recorded. Like the fall, ideas are so subtle and fleeting. I needed some new senses to hear with and see with. That shouldn't be too difficult, I kept telling myself. Autumn is your favorite season - snug and comfortable. While I was on my self-imposed retreat I found these wonderful thoughts on the art of giving which I want to share with you. They are from Letters To My Son by Kent Nerburn.

"Remember to be gentle with yourself and others. We are all children of chance, and none can say why some fields will blossom and others lay brown beneath the August sun. Care for those around you. Look past your differences. Their dreams are no less than yours, their choices in life no more easily made. And give. Give in any way you can, of whatever you possess. To give is to love. To withhold is to wither. Care less for your harvest than how it is shared, and your life will have meaning and your heart will have peace."

Fall is a season of intimate charm and beauty. I love replacing all the brightly colored summer decorations with my favorite fall accents - in colors which I have preferred my entire life - rich in design and hue. The collection of autumnal colors and patterns set my mind spinning! So many quilts to make! Why not go to my scrap bag and grab the first thing I see - chances are that it will go with everything else I like. After all, any fabric chosen with conviction will work with any other fabric.

When I started Quilting in the Country, everything fell into place quickly because I'd spent my lifetime honing my tastes. Up to that point I had focused on raising my children, doing some volunteer work, selling and teaching quilting and patchwork. But with more people leaving the cities, there was a hunger to learn again the lessons of lost arts: quilting, tatting, crochet, woodworking, food preservation and so forth. I wanted to make sure our children (or other people want to make sure their children) would never forget what their grandparents had known. Even in the computer age we are all hungry for learning something that is not high-tech.

My mother-in-law is a wonderful seamstress and has knitted and sewn countless garments in addition to curtains and tablecloths - anything she was asked to do. Recently, Jeanette's failing health had not permitted any sewing. What wonderful news when we learned that she was back to it - making a patchwork table runner for her daughters' redecorated home. Perhaps this will speed her recovery!

Maybe we find our calling amongst scraps of fabric. I love the feel of fabric in my hands - "pinching the goods," as my father-in-law was so fond of saying. Quilting relaxes you. It's doing something for yourself, and it's sure a lot cheaper than a psychologist! Quilting takes your mind off yourself. Seeing how the design and fabrics work together is almost like doing a puzzle. You want to make just one more quilt block or put in just a few more stitches. You become completely absorbed.

As summer departs we emerge ourselves in thoughts of cozy autumn hideaways. Catalogs advertising the perfect Christmas gifts start arriving in the mailbox (how did I get on so many mailing lists?) and we realize that what is created by hand is what is left behind to be cherished by those whose lives you touch.

With changing leaves and cooling temperatures what better time than fall for a trip to Quilting in the Country? It is my hope that our great products will inspire you to take the time to make some special gifts for others and something for yourself, too. Then, we will truly be giving the best of what we have to give to each other - a tangible symbol of our care, concern and love for one another.

Jane

Fruit and Bulgar Salad

Juli Rognlie
Bozeman, Montana

Juli was in elementary school with my daughter, Anne. Now Juli is a very important part of Quilting in the Country. She coordinates our kits and block-of-the-month packets, and also works in the store and teaches. We think she's a perfect fit for us.

3	cups water
1/2	cup yellow split peas
3/4	cup dry bulgar wheat
3/4	cup boiling water
1	cup red apple, chopped
1/4	cup dried cranberries
1/4	cup dates or raisins, chopped
1/4	cup plain yogurt
2	tablespoons lemon juice
1/4	teaspoon curry
1	11-ounce can mandarin oranges
5	tablespoons toasted almonds, chopped

Cook water and peas for 3 minutes, drain. Combine bulgar wheat and boiling water and let set for 30 minutes. Stir all remaining ingredients together, except almonds and chill. Top with almonds before serving.

In order to be really free, let your past go.
Inspirational Concepts in Sulky

Chicken and Wild Rice

Barb Cribb
Bozeman, Montana

Barb's salad makes a great summer meal when served on a bed of lettuce with bread and fresh tomato wedges.

Salad:

1 1/2	cups cooked, diced chicken
3/4	cups celery, chopped
4	cups cooked wild rice
2	cups seedless red grapes
3/4	cup salted cashews or peanuts

Dressing:

mayonnaise

vinegar

sugar

For dressing, mix mayonnaise, vinegar, and sugar to taste. Mix all salad ingredients together in a large bowl, add dressing, and refrigerate until ready to serve.

Rice Salad

Eleanor Christian
Bozeman, Montana

5 cups chicken broth

2 cups uncooked
white rice

3 6-ounce jars marinated
artichokes, chopped
(reserve juice)

1 tablespoon curry powder

2 cups mayonnaise

salt and pepper to taste

5 green onions, chopped

1 4-ounce jar pimento
green olives

1 large green pepper, diced

3 large celery stalks, diced

1/4 cup fresh
parsley, chopped

Cook rice in chicken broth and cool. Mix reserved artichoke marinade with curry powder, mayonnaise, salt, and pepper. Combine remaining ingredients and rice and toss dressing.

Swedish Salad

Lorna Wharrier
Great Britain

I was delighted when this international recipe came in from my friend Lorna. It is somewhat difficult to find fenugreek and garam masala in Bozeman, but I did eventually locate them at our health food store. This salad feeds a lot of people, but it can be made in smaller quantities if desired.

Salad:

1   pound white basmati rice

1   medium chicken, roasted

1   15-ounce can sweet corn, drained

1   red apple, diced

1   green apple, diced

2   bananas, sliced and coated with lemon juice

Curry Mayonnaise:

1   20-ounce jar good-quality mayonnaise

4   cloves, crushed

1   teaspoon cumin seed

1   teaspoon ground coriander

1/2   teaspoon onion seed

1/2   teaspoon ground fenugreek

1/2   teaspoon chili powder

1/2   teaspoon ground ginger

1/2   teaspoon tumeric

1   teaspoon garam masala

    salt

    freshly ground black pepper

Cook rice according to directions, rinse with cold water, drain and leave cool. Roughly shred chicken and add to rice. Add sweet corn and fruit and mix thoroughly. Serve with curry mayonnaise and a green salad of your choice.

Garam Masala means "hot spices" because it is believed to raise body temperature. Although not spicy, the mixture does add fragrant warmth to dishes. It is available from Indian grocers, but you can also make the mix at home: Grind three 4-inch cinnamon sticks, the seeds of 12 cardamom pods, add 6 cloves in a spice grinder, sieving any large pieces. Yields one tablespoon.
— Denver Post

Main Dish Salad

Joyce Slingsby
Bozeman, Montana

This salad is delicious served with your favorite rolls or bread and a small fruit salad. Joyce's mother called this "Garden Rice Salad". Joyce notes that while the recipe makes a lot, it also keeps very well. Knowing my other favorite food is soup, Joyce referred to this recipe as a salad "in lieu" of soup!

2   cloves garlic, minced

1   onion, chopped

2   carrots, chopped

1   celery stalk, chopped

2/3 cup fresh
     parsley, chopped

2   teaspoons dried basil

1   teaspoon dried oregano

2   tomatoes, chopped

1   16-ounce can
     vegetarian baked beans

5   cups cooked rice

1   cup vinegar

2   teaspoons salt (optional)

3/4 teaspoon pepper

Sautè garlic, onion, carrots, celery, parsley, basil, and oregano in a small amount of water until the vegetables are tender. Add tomatoes, beans, and rice. Combine vinegar, salt, and pepper, and toss with the vegetables. Chill overnight before serving.

Serves 12

Nutty Wild Rice Salad

Lyn Housel
Greeley, Colorado

Lyn's recipe for Nutty Wild Rice Salad is often requested and a little unusual.
Lynn has contributed some wonderful quilts to our annual outdoor quilt show.

Salad:

1/2	cup wild rice
1	can (2 cups) beef broth
1	cup frozen peas, thawed
2	stalks celery, thinly sliced
4	green onions, thinly sliced
1/4	cup slivered, toasted almonds
	lettuce leaves

Dressing:

2	tablespoons red wine vinegar
1	tablespoon soy sauce
1	teaspoon sugar
2-3	tablespoons oil

Cover rice with cold water; water should be approximately 1-inch above rice. Heat to boiling. Drain water from rice and add bouillon. Simmer, covered, until all liquid is absorbed, 1 hour or more. Combine all dressing ingredients and mix well. While rice is still warm, toss with dressing. Cool. Add peas, celery, green onions, and almonds. Toss well. Serve on lettuce.

Southwest Rice and Bean Salad

Kathy Doeden
Miles City, Montana

Jicama, celery, or water chestnuts are also nice additions to this salad instead of the peppers.

2 1/2 cups water

1   cup uncooked long grain rice

1   tablespoon instant chicken bouillon, or 3 chicken bouillon cubes

1   15 1/2-ounce can kidney beans, drained

1   cup red bell pepper, coarsely chopped

1   cup green bell pepper, coarsely chopped

1   4-ounce (or more) can chopped mild green chilies, undrained

1/3   cup bottled lemon juice

3   tablespoons vegetable oil

1/2   teaspoon ground cumin

2   tablespoons sugar

1/4   teaspoon garlic powder

Bring water, rice, and bouillon to a boil. Reduce heat, cover, and simmer 15-20 minutes until rice is tender. In a large salad bowl, combine vegetables, chilies, and rice. Mix remaining ingredients and pour over rice mixture. Cover and chill 2-4 hours; overnight is even better. Stir before serving.

8 servings

Taboule Primavera

Eleanor Christian
Bozeman, Montana

Eleanor is a quilting friend from way back. Her applique quilts are stunning.

1	package *Near East Taboule Wheat Salad Mix*
1	cup carrots, shredded
1	cup tomatoes, chopped
1	cup frozen peas
1	cup canned black beans, rinsed and drained
1/4	cup fresh basil, chopped
2	tablespoons lemon juice
1	tablespoon virgin olive oil
	lettuce
	feta cheese

Prepare Taboule as directed on the package. Cover and refrigerate 30 minutes. Stir in remaining ingredients, except cheese. Cover and refrigerate at least 2 hours. Serve on a bed of lettuce and sprinkle with feta cheese.

To appreciate quilts and making them, is to understand their origins and their purpose in earlier times.

Rice-A-Roni Salad

Linda James
Bozeman, Montana

Being a skilled handworker, Linda introduced her mother to quiltmaking after her mother's retirement. Mother and daughter have had lots of fun sharing the love of quilting.

1   box chicken flavored *Rice-A-Roni*

1   6-ounce can tuna fish, drained

1   can water chestnuts, drained

2   stalks celery, sliced

1   tablespoon lemon juice

    Miracle Whip salad dressing

Prepare chicken flavored *Rice-A-Roni* as directed on the box; cool. Mix all ingredients, adding enough *Miracle Whip* to hold the mixture together.

GREEN SALADS

Pansies, roses, Johnny-jump-ups, violets, cornflowers, scented geranium leaves, lavender, hibiscus, nasturtiums, calendula, snapdragons, bachelor buttons, chrysanthemum daisies, margarita daisies, marigolds, and flowering maple blossoms are popular edible flowers.

Flowers are extremely perishable and begin to wilt as soon as they are removed from their stems. If you grow edible varieties yourself, they should be picked as soon as they open. Carefully inspect the flowers for insects and debris, mist lightly with water, and air dry or gently pat dry. Here are a few ideas to get you started:

Add color and flavor to a simple mixed green salad with edible flowers such as nasturtiums, borage, and calendula. Make sure to toss the salad with vinaigrette before adding blossoms to prevent sogginess.

Larger flowers can be used, with petals intact, as elegant containers for simple foods. For a bridal shower, try a blossom filled with crabmeat or tuna salad for an elegant presentation.
— — Martha Stewart, Bozeman Daily Chronicle

Spinach Salad with Tangerines

Marge Sande, "Quilt-A-Way"
Great Falls, Montana

Marge is such a delightful lady. She was one of the early supporters when Quilter's Art Guild of the Northern Rockies was organized.

Salad:

1	pound (about 8 cups) bunch spinach, stems removed
1/4	medium-size red onion, thinly sliced
	rice wine vinegar
2-3	tangerines
1	teaspoon sesame seeds, toasted

Sesame-Ginger Vinaigrette:

1	teaspoon tangerine zest, minced
2	tablespoons fresh tangerine juice
2	teaspoons fresh ginger, grated
2 1/2	tablespoons rice wine vinegar
2	tablespoons light olive oil
1	tablespoon dark sesame oil
1	teaspoon soy sauce
1/4	teaspoon salt

Wash the greens and dry them in a spinner, wrap loosely in a damp towel and refrigerate. Toss the onion with a splash of rice wine vinegar to draw out the pink color. Peel and section the tangerines, removing any seeds, pith, or thread. Make the vinaigrette by combining all ingredients except the tangerine zest in a blender, blending and whisking in the zest. Combine the greens, onions and tangerines in a large bowl. Toss with the vinaigrette and sprinkle with sesame seeds.

4 servings

Strawberry and Spinach Salad

Maryanne Harbour and Jane Quinn
Bozeman, Montana

This is one of my all-time family favorites. I received the recipe many years ago at a "Thank You Salad Luncheon" held at a local elementary school where I had helped with a quilting project.

Salad:

- 1 pound fresh spinach, cleaned
- 1 pint fresh strawberries, sliced (Maryanne sometimes substitutes tangerines or oranges)

Dressing:

- 3 packets artificial sweetener (*Equal*), or 1/2 cup sugar
- 2 tablespoons sesame seed
- 1 tablespoon poppy seed
- 1 1/2 teaspoons dry minced onion
- 1/4 teaspoon Worcestershire sauce
- 1/4 teaspoon paprika
- 1/4 cup cider vinegar
- 1/2 cup salad oil

Shake dressing ingredients well until sugar is dissolved, then add salad oil and shake again.

Pour over spinach and strawberries; toss.

Three-Step Romaine Salad

Sally Cokelet
Bozeman, Montana

Recently Sally and her husband moved back to Bozeman after a twenty-year absence. Sally is learning to quilt after many years as a needle worker.

Salad:

- 1/2 cup sliced almonds (Sally says blanched almonds are much easier to slice)
- 3 tablespoons sugar
- 1 cup Romaine lettuce, torn
- 1 11-ounce can mandarin oranges, drained
- 1 cup celery, sliced
- 3 green onions, sliced

Dressing:

- 1/2 cup oil
- 1/4 cup red wine vinegar
- 2-3 tablespoons sugar
- 1/2 teaspoon salt
- 1/2 teaspoon dry mustard
- 1/2 teaspoon garlic powder

In a small pan over medium heat, cook and stir nuts and sugar until nuts are coated and lightly browned. Spread on foil to cool; gently break apart. In a large bowl, combine lettuce, oranges, celery, and onions. Top with almonds.

In a jar with a tight-fitting lid, combine all dressing ingredients. At the time of serving, shake well, pour over salad, and toss.

Heart of Paradise Salad

Glenda Mitchell
Livingston, Montana

This unusual salad recipe came to Glenda from her friend and quilting pal, Carole Yost, who also lives in the Paradise Valley. Glenda says she had no choice but to call it "Heart of Paradise Salad"! Carole added the avocado; Glenda added the pears. It is luscious-looking on salad plates, but tastes just as yummy from a big salad bowl.

Salad:

1	head leaf lettuce
3	medium navel oranges, peeled and sliced
3	medium pears, cored and sliced
1	small sweet onion
1	avocado, peeled and sliced

Dressing:

1/2	cup vegetable oil
1/4	cup vinegar
4	teaspoons sugar
4	teaspoons poppy seed
1/4	teaspoon salt
	dash of pepper

Shake dressing ingredients together in a small jar. Rinse lettuce and tear into bite-size pieces. Line six salad plates with greens. Arrange orange slices on plates. Top with pear slices and 2-3 onion rings. Garnish with one or two thin slices of avocado. Pass the dressing and enjoy!

Alternate preparation method: Break lettuce into salad bowl. Add oranges, pears, and avocado. Cut into appropriate portions. Add onion. Toss. Dress lightly and serve. To serve as a tossed salad, you may wish to add more lettuce. (Mandarin oranges may be substituted for navel oranges.)

6 servings

Spinach Waldorf Salad

Pat Lorenz
Denver, Colorado

Pat was the secretary at the University of Minnesota Large Animal Clinic when Bill and I first married. We've been friends ever since. Some of my very best recipes have come from Pat.

1/2 cup mayonnaise

2 tablespoons frozen apple juice concentrate

1/4 teaspoon cinnamon

2 red apples, cored and cubed

1/2 cup seedless red grapes, halved

1/2 cup celery, chopped

1/2 cup walnuts, chopped

4 cups fresh spinach leaves, torn

In a large bowl, combine mayonnaise, juice, and cinnamon. Add apples, grapes, celery, and walnuts, tossing to coat. Just before serving, place spinach in a large bowl. Spoon apple mixture over spinach. Toss to mix and coat.

Wilted Leaf Lettuce

Corrine Hoffart
Bozeman, Montana

Being invited to Corrine's home is a special treat - like being invited to the inside of a "Country Living" magazine. This is a delightful last-minute salad when you have fresh lettuce in your garden. The recipe can be found in pioneer cookbooks; those ladies had these ingredients. It is still a special salad. Cut your leaf lettuce early in the morning, wash, putting a paper towel in the bottom of a bowl and a dampened towel on top to make these lettuce leaves crisp!

2	large bunches leaf lettuce
	salt and pepper, to taste
2	teaspoons sugar
2	green onions, sliced
4	slices bacon
1/4	cup salad vinegar
2	tablespoons water
2	hard-cooked eggs, quartered

Tear lettuce into a bowl, season with salt and pepper; add sugar and onion. Fry bacon crisp, crumble. Add vinegar and water to drippings, heat to boiling and pour over lettuce. Toss until wilted. Add bacon and eggs. Eat this salad while it is still warm.

4 servings

No one can arrive from being talented alone.
God gives talent: work transforms talent into genius.

Raspberry Pecan Salad with Poppy Seed Dressing

Kathy Center
Bozeman, Montana

Serve this with a nice quiche and hot rolls and you will have a luncheon fit for a queen. Kathy works at Quilting in the Country and we know everything she does is first class!

Salad:

- 8 cups mixed salad greens, including Boston lettuce
- 1 cup fresh raspberries
- 1 large avocado, sliced
- 1/2 pound fresh mushrooms, sliced
- 1/2 cup pecans (may be candied)
- edible flowers

Dressing:

- 1/2 cup raspberry spreadable fruit
- 1/3 cup raspberry vinegar
- 1 tablespoon honey
- 1 tablespoon poppy seed
- 1/3 cup canola oil

Wash greens and refrigerate until ready to serve. Combine ingredients for dressing with a whisk or blender. Put greens in a bowl, top with remaining salad ingredients, and toss with dressing. Garnish with edible flowers.

Sharon's Famous Bleu Cheese Salad

Sharon Burkhalter
Bozeman, Montana

Sharon and I shared car-pooling to nursery school. Now we're both grand-moms!

Salad:

1	head Romaine lettuce
1	clove fresh garlic, minced
2-3	tablespoons olive oil
2-3	tablespoons fresh lemon juice
1/2	4-ounce package bleu cheese (use whole package if preferred)
	parmesan cheese
	red bell pepper slices (optional)
	salt and pepper, to taste

Toss lettuce and garlic. Drizzle olive oil over salad, toss, and add lemon juice. Sprinkle with cheese and a dash of salt and pepper.

Lettuce Salad

Nancy K. Hall, "Quilt-A-Way"
Great Falls, Montana

1	head lettuce, chopped
1	small box frozen peas, cooked
1	green pepper, finely chopped
1	pint mayonnaise
1/2	pound fried bacon, crumbled or chopped into small pieces (use 3/4 cup if preferred)
	parmesan cheese

In a 9 X 12 inch cake pan, layer the following ingredients as follows: lettuce, warm cooked peas, and green pepper. Seal these three ingredients with the mayonnaise. Next, top the mayonnaise with the bacon and cover with parmesan cheese. Let stand overnight in the refrigerator before serving.

Bleu Cheese, Tomato, and Iceberg Lettuce

Anne Quinn Egan
Denver, Colorado

My daughter, Anne, adapted this recipe from a salad served at Sullivan's Steakhouse in Denver. It is very rich!

Salad:

    bleu cheese, crumbled

    tomato, diced

    iceberg lettuce,
    cut into wedges

Dressing:

1	cup mayonnaise
1	pound bleu cheese, crumbled
1/2	cup sour cream
3/4	cup heavy cream
2	tablespoons lemon juice
1	teaspoon lemon zest
2	teaspoons salt
1 1/2	teaspoons freshly ground black pepper

To make dressing, combine mayonnaise, about 3/4 pound of the bleu cheese, sour cream, heavy cream, and lemon juice in a food processor or blender. Process until smooth. Transfer the mixture to a mixing bowl and add remaining bleu cheese, lemon zest, salt, and pepper. Adjust seasoning and refrigerate for at least one hour.

For salad, distribute wedges of lettuce on each of four salad plates. Top with bleu cheese crumbles and diced tomatoes. Drizzle generously with bleu cheese dressing. Serve.

Color Splash Salad

Pat Paynich
Bozeman, Montana

As you might guess, Pat is a very talented friend. Since Pat has become acquainted with the color wheel over the years, she looks at salad fruits and vegetables in relation to color. She wanders the fresh produce section of the supermarket looking at color and value. As a result, the idea for Color Splash Salad was born. The bonus with this salad is a wholesome dish high in beta carotene and fiber to tackle all those "bad" free radicals in the body, not to mention a variety of sumptuous taste sensations.

Since the variety of fresh fruits and vegetables changes seasonally, Pat has only a master plan to follow and she tries to incorporate all the families of the color wheel as a guide. Some of Pat's examples include:

Yellow - bell pepper, squash, carrots, mandarin oranges, marigolds

Red - cabbage, strawberries, raspberries, radishes, radicchio, beets (cooked), rose petals

Blue - pepper, blueberries, pansies

Green - celery, cucumber, Chinese pea pods, green beans, cabbage, asparagus

To assemble a Color Splash Salad, chop a 1/2 cup of each of 8-10 vegetables and/or fruits, incorporating a variety of colors. Mix vegetables and fruits into a bowl of fresh Romaine or red leaf lettuce. "Dress" as desired. Pat uses Rice Wine Dressing (recipe follows), or a fruit-flavored vinaigrette. Adding a 1/2 cup nuts is also a tasty option for this salad.

Rice Wine Dressing:

1 tablespoon light olive oil

1/2 cup rice wine vinegar

1 teaspoon sugar

1/2 teaspoon salt

Dissolve sugar and salt in rice vinegar. Add olive oil. Mix together; serve over salad.

Spinach Salad

Lois Christiansen
Bismarck, North Dakota

Salad:

1	package fresh spinach
3	hard-boiled eggs, chopped
6	strips crisp bacon, crumbled
1	can bean sprouts, drained
1	can water chestnuts, drained and sliced

Dressing:

1	cup salad oil
1/2	cup ketchup
1	teaspoon Worcestershire sauce
3/4	cup vinegar
3/4	cup sugar
1	small onion

Wash spinach well and drain. Combine all salad ingredients and toss just before serving. Blend dressing ingredients. Refrigerate until ready to serve. Serve dressing with salad.

Serves 8

Spinach, Orange, and Walnut Salad

Bonnie Pascucci
Billings Montana

For Bonnie's recipe, toast walnuts in an oven, microwave, or dry fry pan until they smell good and start to darken.

Salad:

1	pound mixed greens or spinach
1/2	red onion, thinly sliced
1	cup radishes, thinly sliced
1	cup walnuts, toasted
3	teaspoons olive oil
	salt and pepper, to taste

Dressing:

6	oranges
1	tablespoon honey
1/2	teaspoon cinnamon

At least one hour before serving, peel and section the oranges. Peel membranes off each section. Cut orange sections into halves. Drizzle with honey and cinnamon and let sit.

While oranges rest, clean greens and dry. Combine greens with onion, radishes, and nuts. Toss with olive oil. Season with salt and pepper. Just before serving, add oranges and all their juices. Toss to mix well.

Some people make the world more special just by being in it.

Spinach Strawberry Salad

Diane Towers
Bozeman, Montana

This is Diane's favorite salad in June when the strawberries and spinach are garden-ready. For a winter variation, substitute one head torn Romaine lettuce for the spinach and a can of mandarin oranges for the strawberries.

Salad:

4-6	cups fresh spinach, torn
1/4	cup red onion, diced
2	cups strawberry halves
8-10	large mushrooms, sliced
1/3	cup toasted, slivered almonds

Dressing:

1/2	cup salad oil
1/3	cup honey
2	tablespoons vinegar
2	teaspoons poppy seed
1/2	teaspoon dry mustard
1/2	teaspoon salt

For dressing, combine oil, honey, vinegar, poppy seed, mustard, and salt in a small bowl. Beat until well mixed. Transfer to a shaker jar and refrigerate several hours to blend the flavors.

In large bowl, combine spinach, onion, strawberries, mushrooms, and almonds. Just before serving, shake dressing and pour over salad, tossing until thoroughly coated.

Serves 4 to 6

Spinach Salad

Eva Veltkamp
Bozeman, Montana

Eva and I have shared the love of quilting for a long time. We even team-taught Beginning Quiltmaking!

Salad:

1   package fresh spinach, washed and chopped

1   can water chestnuts, drained and sliced

8-10 slices bacon, cut small and fried crisp

1/2 pound fresh mushrooms, washed and sliced

3   hard-boiled eggs, peeled and sliced

Dressing:

1   small onion, chopped

1/2 cup ketchup

1/2 cup vinegar

2   teaspoons salt

1/2 cup vegetable oil

3/4 cup sugar

1   tablespoon Worcestershire sauce

Put dressing ingredients in a jar, cover with plastic wrap, screw on lid, and shake well until mixed. Mix salad ingredients and toss with dressing. Refrigerate any remaining dressing.

Romaine and Strawberry Salad with Poppy Seed Dressing

Lynda Faulkner
Helena, Montana

Lynda was shopping in the store one afternoon when I asked her for special salad recipes. She was nice enough to send this recipe, as well as two salad dressing recipes.

Salad:

1	head Romaine lettuce, torn into bite-size pieces (can also use spinach, etc.)
1	pint strawberries, sliced
1/2	red onion, thinly sliced

Dressing:

1/2	cup mayonnaise
1/3	cup sugar
2	tablespoons vinegar
1/4	cup milk
1	tablespoon poppy seed

Combine dressing ingredients and mix well. Pour over salad just before serving and toss lightly.

Creole Tomato and Heart of Palm Salad

Jan Rutledge
Bozeman, Montana

Salad:

2   heads red leaf lettuce

4   large tomatoes,
    cut in wedges

2   cans heart of palm,
    drained and cut into
    small rounds

9   fresh basil leaves,
    snipped, or 1 tablespoon
    dried basil

1/2 pound Roquefort or
     bleu cheese, crumbled

Dressing:

1/2 cup plus 1 tablespoon
     olive oil

1/4 cup red wine vinegar

1   tablespoon Dijon
     mustard

1/2 teaspoon salt

1/2 teaspoon cracked pepper

1   teaspoon sugar

2   garlic cloves, minced

For dressing, whisk 1 tablespoon oil with vinegar, mustard, salt, pepper, sugar, and garlic. Whisk in remaining oil in a thin stream.

Tear lettuce into bite-sized pieces. Combine with tomatoes, heart of palm, and basil in a salad bowl. Toss with dressing and sprinkle with cheese.

Ronni's Strawberry Salad

Cheryl Wittmayer - "Sew Be It"
Billings, Montana

One of our most popular Block-of-the-Month patterns is Cheryl's Nostalgia Garden. Cheryl's recipe for Ronni's Strawberry Salad goes with her challenge block. She calls the salad ingredients a bit odd, but says it's unbelievably yummy and not just for ladies, either!

Salad:

1/4	cup chopped pecans (use 1/2 cup if preferred)
1/8	teaspoon cinnamon
1	pound spinach leaves, cleaned and dried, chopped if preferred
	red onion, sliced
24	fresh strawberries, sliced

Dressing:

1	cup sugar
1 1/2	teaspoons dry mustard
1/2	cup cider vinegar
1 1/2	teaspoons salt
1	cup plus 3 tablespoons salad oil
2-3	teaspoons poppy seed

Bake pecans and cinnamon for 5 minutes at 350 degrees. Toss pecans with other salad ingredients.

Heat sugar, dry mustard, cider vinegar, and salt until sugar is dissolved. Stir in oil and poppy seed. Chill. (Dressing will blend together and thicken while chilling.) To serve, drizzle dressing over room temperature salad.

Pear, Bleu Cheese, and Walnut Salad

Corrine Hoffart
Bozeman, Montana

I was pleasantly surprised when Corrine submitted this recipe. My daughter, Anne, also makes this salad and we've eaten it on more than one occasion at her house. Anne uses Newman's Own salad dressing on her salad, but the Pear-Nectar Vinaigrette sounds great for a sweeter variation.

3	medium pears
2	tablespoons lemon juice
2	ounces (1/2 cup) bleu cheese, crumbled
	candied walnuts or pecans (see recipe below)
	Pear-Nectar Vinaigrette (see Dressings)
	mixed salad greens

Halve and core pears. Thinly slice pears; brush with lemon juice to prevent browning. (This may be done up to one hour ahead.)

To arrange salads, line plates with salad greens. Fan pear slices atop each serving. Sprinkle with some crumbled cheese and candied walnuts or pecans. Use only 3/4 cup Pear-Nectar Vinaigrette to drizzle over all, reserve the rest for another use.

8 side-dish servings

Candied Walnuts or Pecans

Corrine Hoffart
Bozeman, Montana

1	cup walnuts
1/2	cup sugar
2	tablespoons margarine or butter

Line a baking sheet with foil. Butter the foil; set aside. In a heavy 10-inch skillet over medium-high heat, cook the walnuts, sugar, and butter, shaking skillet occasionally until sugar begins to melt. Do not stir. Reduce heat to low and cook until sugar is golden brown, stirring occasionally. Remove from heat. Pour onto the prepared baking sheet. Cool completely and break into clusters.

Makes about 10-ounces

Avocado and Hearts of Palm Salad

Doreen Ratzburg
Shelby, Montana

Salad:

1   large ripe avocado, peeled and sliced

1   14-ounce can hearts of palm, drained and sliced

1   head Romaine lettuce, torn in bite-size pieces

Herb Dressing:

1/3   cup olive oil

1/4   teaspoon dried basil leaves

3   tablespoons wine vinegar

1   tablespoon onion, chopped

1/8   teaspoon powdered thyme

1   tablespoon water

1/8   teaspoon powdered marjoram

1 /2   teaspoon salt

1   tablespoon parsley, chopped

Combine all dressing ingredients in a blender. Blend for about 10 seconds. Combine salad ingredients and toss well with dressing.

Serves 6 - 8

Layered Chef's Salad

Shannon Heffern
Scottsdale, Arizona

1 1/2 cups water

1/2 cup quick barley

1-2 teaspoons soy sauce

2 tablespoons butter or margarine

4 cups lettuce greens, torn

2 cups ham and/or chicken, cooked and cubed

1 cup green, red, or yellow peppers, chopped

1 cup celery, chopped

1/2 cup carrots, shredded

1 1/4 cup mayonnaise

2 tablespoons prepared mustard

1 tablespoon sugar

1 teaspoon dill weed

2 eggs, hard-boiled

1 cup (4-ounces) cheddar cheese, grated

1/4 cup green onion, sliced

Cook barley in boiling water, 10-12 minutes. Drain. In fry pan, saute barley in soy sauce and butter until browned and beginning to pop. Cool.

In a large clear serving bowl, layer lettuce, ham or chicken, peppers, barley, celery, and carrots. Combine mayonnaise, mustard, sugar, and dill weed. Mix well. Spoon mayonnaise mixture over top of salad, spreading to edges of bowl.

Slice eggs and place over dressing. Sprinkle cheese and green onion on top. Cover with plastic wrap and refrigerate several hours or overnight.

Toss salad just before serving.

6-8 main dish servings

Autumn Salad

Rose McCaig
Pointe Claire, Quebec, Canada

Salad:

2	heads butter lettuce
1/2	red onion, diced
1	4-ounce package bleu cheese, crumbled
1	Granny Smith apple, diced
1/2	cup pecans or walnuts, chopped
1/2	cup dried cranberries

Raspberry Vinaigrette:

1/3	cup raspberry jam
1/4	cup olive or canola oil
4	teaspoons rice vinegar
4	teaspoons cider vinegar, or 8-ounces raspberry vinegar
1	teaspoon coarse-grind mustard or 1/2 teaspoon dry mustard

Toss all salad ingredients. Pour blended vinaigrette over salad.

Mandarin Orange Salad

Tracy Kimball
Bozeman, Montana

Luzann Bennett submitted this recipe on behalf of Tracy Kimball. Luzann says that Gorgonzola cheese also works well, as do grated carrots.

2   bags Romaine lettuce
1   large can mandarin oranges, drained
1   medium bag almond slivers
2   avocados, sliced
1/2 bottle *Brianna's Homestyle Poppy Seed Dressing* (plus a splash)
1   cup crumbled bleu cheese

Toast almonds at 300 degrees for 5-10 minutes. Toss all ingredients and serve.

Wilted Salad

Linda Snedigar
Billings, Montana

1/2 pound fried bacon, chopped
1/2 cup wine vinegar
1   head Romaine lettuce (or 1 package fresh spinach)
1/2 medium red onion, sliced in rings
1/4 pound fresh mushrooms (use 1/2 cup if preferred)
    generous amounts salt, pepper, and garlic salt
1   hard-boiled egg, grated

Fry bacon, remove from pan, and add wine vinegar to grease. Heat vinegar mixture to bubbling, season heavily, and add bacon again. Pour mixture over mixed salad while grease is warm. Sprinkle egg over salad if desired.

Serves 6

Caesar Salad

Corrine Hoffart
Bozeman, Montana

Corrine calls this a "quick" Caesar with an "oil spill" - olive, of course!

Salad:

1 head Romaine lettuce, torn into bite-sized pieces

croutons

parmesan cheese

Dressing:

2 teaspoons fresh garlic, minced

2 anchovies

1 tablespoon Worcestershire sauce

2 teaspoons Dijon mustard

1 tablespoon parmesan cheese, grated

1/4 cup water

1 tablespoon lemon juice

freshly ground black pepper

1/2 cup olive oil

For dressing, combine all ingredients except olive oil in a blender. With motor running, slowly pour olive oil into blender and process until the dressing emulsifies. Adjust seasoning.

For salad, toss lettuce with the dressing and divide among four dinner plates. Sprinkle with croutons and additional parmesan cheese. Serve.

Trash Bag Salad

Trish Foster
Bozeman, Montana

Trish is my favorite non-cooking friend. She wants to build her new home with a drive-up window rather than a kitchen!

Salad:

1	head Romaine lettuce
1/2	cup sliced almonds
1	cup mandarin oranges

Dressing:

1/4	cup sugar (use 1/2 cup if preferred)
1/3	cup vegetable oil
1	tablespoon mustard
2	tablespoons poppy seed
1/4	cup vinegar
1	teaspoon salt

Mix dressing ingredients. Tear lettuce into a clean trash bag. Add almonds and mandarin oranges. Pour in dressing and shake.

Holiday Green Salad

Jane Quinn
Bozeman, Montana

Salad:

6	cups iceberg lettuce, torn
6	cups Romaine lettuce, torn
3	green onions, thinly sliced
1	celery rib, thinly sliced
3/4	cup dried cranberries (use 1 cup if preferred)
1/4	cup sliced almonds, toasted

Dressing:

1/4	cup vegetable oil
1/4	cup vinegar
1/4	cup sugar
1	tablespoon fresh parsley, minced
1/2	teaspoon hot pepper sauce (use 1 teaspoon if preferred)
1/4	teaspoon salt

For salad, combine greens, onions, and celery in a large bowl. In a small bowl, combine dressing ingredients; mix well. Pour dressing over salad and toss to coat. Add cranberries and almonds. Serve immediately.

Serves 10-12

Parents give their children two gifts ...
one is roots and the other is wings.

MacKenzie River House Salad

Maria Wolslagel
Bozeman, Montana

Maria's favorite "House Salad" is the salad that the guys and gals at MacKenzie River Pizza Company toss together. The General Manager, Noel Ellis, tells her that the dressing is a "secret recipe". It's taste hints of raspberry. Try it! You may like it!

Salad:

> medley of crisp Romaine and red leaf lettuce, tossed with chopped red cabbage
>
> shredded carrots
>
> D'Anjou pears with skin, cut in wedges

Top salad ingredients with a sprinkle of Grapenuts cereal and a dressing of "dazzling spicy vinaigrette".

Spinach Salad

Diane Towers
Bozeman, Montana

1/4	cup granulated sugar
1/4	teaspoon salt
1 1/2	teaspoons cornstarch
1/3	cup water
2	tablespoons vinegar
2	egg yolks, beaten
1	cup mayonnaise
1/2	cup red onion, chopped
1/2	pound bacon, fried crisp
2-3	hard-boiled eggs, finely chopped
1	pound fresh spinach

Mix sugar, salt, and cornstarch in a small saucepan; add water & vinegar, then egg yolks. Cook over low heat until thick, stirring constantly; cool slightly. Add mayonnaise to this mixture. Mix in onion, bacon crumbled into bits, and chopped eggs. Refrigerate until well chilled. Wash, stem, and dry spinach. Toss with dressing just before serving.

Serves 8

Puckerbrush Road Salad

Bonnie Tyro
Polson, Montana

We always love it when Bonnie, our sales rep from United Notions, comes to show us all the great new Moda fabric.

Salad:

1	green bell pepper, sliced in rings
1	bunch red leaf lettuce
1	11-ounce can mandarin oranges, drained
1	cup mushrooms
1	small red onion
2	avocados , slice 1 1/2 and mash remainder

Dressing:

1/2	cup mayonnaise
1/2	cup sour cream
1/4	cup dill pickle juice
1	tablespoon fresh parsley
1	teaspoon chives, chopped
1 1/2	teaspoons dill weed

Mix green pepper, lettuce, oranges, mushrooms, onion and avocado.

Make dressing with remaining ingredients, including mashed avocado. Toss vegetables and dressing together.

Green and Orange Salad

Lucille Allen
Sandpoint, Idaho

Orange peel and juice make zesty dressing additions to this salad. Kathy Conger's mother, Lucille Allen, got this recipe from Kathy's cousin who lives in Juneau, Alaska. Kathy's cousin likes to serve it with freshly-caught fish like halibut! We are so lucky to have Kathy on our staff at Quilting in the Country when she takes a day away from her "real" job in a dental office.

2	large oranges
2/3	cup salad oil
3	tablespoons white wine vinegar
1	teaspoon salt
1	teaspoon dry mustard
4	teaspoons sugar
	dash of white pepper
1	tablespoon orange rind, grated (reserve for dressing)
1	small head Romaine lettuce, washed and dried
1	large head butter lettuce, washed and dried
1	small cucumber, peeled, and thinly sliced
3	green onions, thinly sliced

Cut peel and membrane from oranges, slice over bowl to collect juices. Mix salad oil, vinegar, salt, mustard, sugar, pepper, orange peel, and 2 tablespoons reserved orange juice. Tear Romaine and butter lettuce into bite-size pieces to make 14 cups total. In a large bowl, combine lettuces, cucumber, onion, and orange pieces. Toss with dressing.

Serves 6

Mandarin Salad

Malinda Ringo
Denver, Colorado

Malinda's mother, Lois, lives in Bozeman. Malinda reports that her Denver neighbors really liked the <u>Soup's On</u> cookbook.

Salad:
- 1/2 cup almonds, sliced
- 3 tablespoons sugar
- 1/2 head iceberg lettuce
- 1/2 head Romaine lettuce
- 1 cup celery, chopped
- 2 whole green onions, chopped
- 1 11-ounce can mandarin oranges

Dressing:
- 1/2 teaspoon salt
- 1/4 cup vegetable oil
- 1 tablespoon parsley, chopped
- 2 tablespoons sugar
- 2 tablespoons vinegar
- dash Tabasco sauce
- dash pepper

In a small pan over medium heat, cook almonds and sugar until almonds are coated, cool. Mix all dressing ingredients and chill. Mix lettuce, celery, and onions. Before serving, add almonds and oranges. Toss with the dressing and serve.

Serves 4-6

Simply Spring Salad

Carla Farnam
Bozeman, Montana

Carla tells me that this salad is very simple and it certainly contains some of the foods that remind me most of spring - fresh lettuce and strawberries.

Salad:

1   bunch green leaf lettuce, torn

1   pint strawberries, sliced

1   small red onion, thinly sliced

Dressing:

1/4 cup honey

1/3 cup oil

2   tablespoons vinegar

1/4 teaspoon salt

2   teaspoons poppy seed

Combine lettuce, strawberries, and onions in a large salad bowl. Mix dressing and pour over salad. Toss and serve.

We are always the same age inside.
Stein

Caesar Pleaser

Geri Campbell, "All In Stitches"
Polson, Montana

Add your favorite seafood or meat to this salad for an added treat. Serve with hot French bread and a glass of white wine. A wonderful salad for summer.

1   large head Romaine lettuce

1 1/2 tablespoons olive oil

2   large lemons

1   heaping tablespoon garlic, minced

1 1/2 tablespoons parmesan cheese

Wash lettuce and dry on paper towels. Pour oil into bowl. Slice lemon in half and squeeze juice through strainer into bowl. Add garlic and stir all three together. Shred lettuce by hand into large bite-sized pieces. (Cutting the lettuce with a knife tends to make it brown more quickly at the cut.) Toss lettuce with oil, garlic, and lemon juice. Top with parmesan cheese.

HEARTY
SALADS

Ever Dear Quilters-

The moments you remember are written in time.......tiny, little marks, the passing seconds made on your heart, in hopes you can feel them going by, again.....in the future. ~H. Miller

It all started out rather innocently ~ for months I had been thinking about change.After all, what better time? The millennium, and all......

I'm really resistant to change. I hate it when my favorite pair of green shoes has to be replaced. I _never_ want to change hairdressers as that would mean fried hair after the first perm and retraining of the hairdresser. Usually I don't even consult the menu on our Sunday morning brunch outings. I just order my favorite -Huevos Rancheros.

So when I journeyed to Denver to care for my one and half year old grandson last fall I didn't think of it as a time of great reflection. Maybe my original resistance to the request to come to Denver should have been a clue.All sorts of excuses came to mind.How could I possibly reschedule classes? I was responsible for teaching and a trip to the Midwest was planned for a family wedding and a visit with my mother-in-law.... My mind was spinning. But finally I said, I _must_ _change_ my plans and go help out while my three year old granddaughter is hospitalized and recovering from surgery.

Amazingly, the time away gave me time to contemplate. I have a close friend who is always planning her life away, I think. When Easter brunch is finished she is planning Christmas dinner! My friend and I are quite open about our personality differences. She tells me I live in the past, while of course I think I'm firmly rooted in the present.

When little Quinn came home from the hospital I thought a sponge bath was the best alternative for cleansing. We engaged in a conversation about what it was like when Grammy was a little girl visiting her grandparents. Those were the days when a sponge bath meant heating the bath water on the old cooking range which had been converted to use corn cobs as fuel. Then a more graphic description followed of how body temperatures were taken back then before digital thermometers. And even more amazing, the country doctor would sometimes arrive by horse and buggy across the snow covered fields from my grandparents farm to our place when we could not get out for medical treatment! Then Quinn and I continued our discussion about the days before electric washers and clothes dryers and disposable diapers. (I was feeling ancient and I'm sure little Quinn was convinced Grammy was at least a hundred years old!) Changes, Changes, Changes!

In response to this momentous stock-taking occasion, the new millennium, I've been contemplating what this coming century will bring. We have now arrived at the transition into an unimaginable future and I hunger for stability; of continuity with what has gone before. For me that will mean passed-down anecdotes like the ones Quinn and I shared, and treasured quilts, favorite recipes, well-loved furniture, and photographs. These stories and keepsakes offer us reassuring symbols of rootedness. Will we be faced with amazing new physical and psychological changes? Maybe, but my hope is to bridge the gap between yesterday and tomorrow by sharing some of my quilt making passion, making some quilts, and telling my grandchildren some tales of the bygone days, whenever they'll listen!

P.S. Several years ago I stopped making New Years Resolutions. Why should I bother ~ I never kept them anyway? This year is going to be different. I lost two very special friends this fall. Mary Reilly, a woman who befriended our family when we moved to Bozeman, and my high school home economics teacher, Jan Andersen. Both touched and changed my life in immeasurable ways. They were unconditional in their support and love. My goal is to be that for someone in my life.......And on another sad note, Bill and I lost our cat, Patches, this fall. She was very special to us and many of you _knew_ Patches.

Jane

Sesame Shrimp Salad

Marian Neill
Whitehall, Montana

When Marian has a recipe in her file, you know it is good!

Topping:

1	tablespoon butter
1/2	cup slivered almonds
1	3-ounce package ramen noodles
1/3	cup sesame seeds

Salad:

1	cup green onions, thinly sliced
3	heads butter lettuce, cut into bite-sized pieces
1	pound shrimp, cooked and shelled
	celery, sliced (optional)
	carrots, grated (optional)

Dressing:

1/2	cup rice vinegar
1/4	cup vegetable oil
3	tablespoons brown sugar
1	teaspoon soy sauce
2	teaspoons Asian sesame oil

For topping, melt butter in a skillet over medium-high heat. Add noodles, almonds and sesame seeds. Cook, stirring often, until light golden, about 5 minutes. Transfer to paper towels to cool.

Stir dressing ingredients to blend. Toss with salad ingredients. Mix in topping very last.

As I grow older the simple pleasures of life become even more important.

Beef Salad

Marian Neill
Whitehall, Montana

What a blessing it is to have a friend who is a kindred spirit! Two days a month I write Marian's name on my calendar. We try to let nothing interfere with our quilting time. Marian days, I call them!

1/4 cup red wine vinegar

1/4 cup water

2 tablespoons lemon juice

2 tablespoons sugar

1/4 teaspoon dillweed

1/2 teaspoon salt

    pepper

3 cups (about 12-ounces) cold roast beef, cut in strips

1 small onion, thinly sliced

1 head Romaine lettuce

1 cup sour cream

    artichoke hearts

    tomato wedges

Simmer the first 7 ingredients for 15 minutes. Cool. Combine with beef and onion, and chill for several hours or overnight. Drain, reserving the marinade. Break up lettuce; top with beef and onion. Combine sour cream with the reserved marinade. Toss with lettuce and beef. Garnish with artichoke hearts and tomato wedges.

Shrimp Luncheon Salad

Jan Rutledge
Bozeman, Montana

In no time at all, Jan has become a wonderful quilter and like so many quilters, she's a great cook, too.

Salad:

3	hard-boiled eggs, chopped
1	cup celery, finely chopped
1/2	cup ripe olives, chopped
1	small jar pimento, chopped
1	can crabmeat
2	cans medium shrimp, or 1/2-pound fresh salad shrimp
1	large can chow mein noodles

Dressing:

1	4-ounce package whipped cream cheese
1 1/2	cups mayonnaise
1/4	cup chili sauce
3	tablespoons lemon juice
3	drops *Tabasco* sauce
	dash of garlic salt and salt

Gently mix all salad ingredients except chow mein noodles. Store in a closed container in refrigerator overnight. Blend dressing ingredients and refrigerate overnight. Before serving, mix dressing into salad ingredients. Serve over noodles.

Serves 8

Asparagus and Brat Salad

Jane Quinn
Bozeman, Montana

This has been a family favorite for a very long time. It combines two of my favorite ingredients, asparagus and bratwurst.

1	pound fresh asparagus, slightly steamed
8	ounces spaghetti
1/2	teaspoon dried basil
1/2	teaspoon dried thyme, crushed
1	pound fully cooked smoked bratwurst, bias-sliced into 1/2-inch pieces
2	tomatoes, cut into wedges
2	green onions, sliced
3/4	cup Caesar or Italian salad dressing
	grated parmesan cheese

In separate saucepans, cook asparagus and spaghetti according to package directions, drain. Chill separately in ice water for 5 minutes, drain. Toss the spaghetti with the basil and thyme. Add the asparagus, bratwurst, tomatoes, green onions, and salad dressing. Toss lightly. Cover mixture and chill in the freezer 10 to 15 minutes. Before serving, sprinkle the salad with parmesan cheese.

4 servings

Winter, a lingering season, is a time to gather golden moments, embark upon a sentimental journey and enjoy every idle hour.
John Boswell

Tuna, Barley, and Black Bean Salad

Sally Creeny
Boulder, Colorado

This is fast, good for you, and leaves lots of time to sew!

Salad:

1   cup quick cooking pearled barley

1   16-ounce can black beans, rinsed

1   small red pepper, finely chopped

2   cups Romaine lettuce, thinly sliced

1   6 1/2-ounce can chunk light tuna, drained

Dressing:

3   tablespoons vegetable oil

2   tablespoons white vinegar

2   teaspoons peeled ginger, grated

2   teaspoons soy sauce

1/4   teaspoon garlic, minced

Cook barley in 2 cups water as directed on the box. Cool, stirring occasionally. Whisk dressing ingredients in a large bowl until blended. Add remaining ingredients and toss gently to mix and coat.

Great opportunities await
those who give more
than what is asked.
Put the uncommon touch
on even the most common task.
We may never have the
opportunity to do great things
in a great way, but we all have
the chance to do small things
in a great way.

After Easter Egg Salad

Mary Robbins
Bozeman, Montana

We are so fortunate to have Mary as a teacher at Quilting in the Country. Her quilting ideas are <u>amazing</u> and her work is impeccable.

8	hard-boiled Easter eggs (plain hard-boiled works, too)
1/2	cup mayonnaise
2	teaspoons curry powder
2	tablespoons black olives, finely chopped
2	tablespoons green onion, finely chopped
	salt and pepper to taste

Peel and chop the eggs. Add the rest of ingredients and mix together. This recipe makes four to five egg salad sandwiches - great on dark rye with sprouts, tomatoes, lettuce, and whatever else you desire.

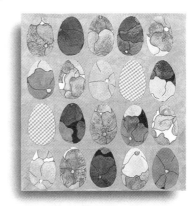

Shrimp Salad

Ruth McIntyre
Helena, Montana

Ruth serves this with a horseradish sauce made from mayonnaise, canned milk, horseradish, and whatever else turns her on.

1	package lemon gelatin
1	cup hot tomato juice
1	cup cold water
1	tablespoon vinegar
1	7-ounce can shrimp
1/2	cup celery, diced
1	tablespoon onion, minced

Combine the first four ingredients and cool in the refrigerator until almost set. Add shrimp, celery, and onion and let set until firm.

Serves 6

Salmon Mousse Salad

Kathy Center
Bozeman, Montana

Kathy uses a fish mold to make this delectable salad. She cautions that if you bring this salad to a potluck, they will never let you bring anything else!

1	envelope unflavored gelatin
1/4	cup water
1/2	cup chicken broth
2	tablespoons fresh dill, or 1 tablespoon dried dill
1/2	cup mayonnaise
1	tablespoon lemon juice
2	small green onions, finely chopped
1/2	teaspoon paprika
1	teaspoon salt
2	cups cooked salmon, finely flaked
1	cup heavy cream
	fresh parsley (for garnish)

Oil a 1 1/2 quart mold. In a large bowl, sprinkle gelatin over 1/4 cup of water and let stand until softened. Add boiling chicken broth and stir until dissolved. Stir in chopped fresh dill and let cool for 10 minutes. Add mayonnaise, lemon juice, green onions, paprika, and salt. Whisk well and refrigerate 20-30 minutes until mixture starts to thicken. Add flaked salmon; mix well and taste for seasoning.

In a separate bowl, beat heavy cream until stiff, and gently fold into the salmon mixture. Pour into the mold and refrigerate at least 2 hours (overnight is best) until firm. Serve on a large platter and surround the salmon with fresh parsley for garnish.

That Taco Salad

Kathy Doeden
Miles City, Montana

Kathy jokes that this salad is not politically or nutritionally correct, but Yummy!

- 1 head iceberg lettuce, cut into bite-size pieces
- 1 large yellow onion, finely chopped
- 1 large tomato, finely chopped
- 1 large avocado, finely chopped (optional)
- 1 7-ounce can mild green chilies, diced
- 1 pound *Velveeta* cheese
- 2 tablespoons milk
- 1 medium bag big *Fritos* or tortilla chips

Mix first five ingredients together. Melt cheese with milk and have a helper slowly pour this over the salad while you mix it together. Without a helper, there is a tendency to clump. (Just before serving, crush *Fritos* or tortilla chips and add to vegetables.)

Easy Crab Salad

Jean Dolan
Bozeman, Montana

- 7-9 slices white bread
- 1 small onion, chopped
- 1 cup celery, chopped
- 1 can crabmeat, flaked (can use imitation crabmeat)
- 2 cans shrimp
- 4 hard-boiled eggs, chopped
- 2 cups (approximately) mayonnaise

Cut crust off bread and cube. Mix with onion and celery. Let stand overnight. Before serving, add crabmeat and shrimp, and eggs and mayonnaise as needed. Chill and serve. (This is also good using all crabmeat.)

Confetti Salad

Gwen Marshall
Australia

Gwen is now living in Bozeman and brings expert needleworking skills from Australia.

3   ounces butter

1   medium onion, finely chopped

5   cups cooked rice

2   chicken stock cubes, crumbled

2   tablespoons ketchup

1   red or green pepper, cut into strips

2   sticks celery, sliced

8   ounces ham, cut into cubes

8   ounces peeled prawns

    mayonnaise to serve (optional)

Melt butter in a frying pan and fry onion until soft and golden. Add rice, chicken cubes, and ketchup to pan and stir thoroughly over medium heat for 2 - 3 minutes. Add pepper, celery, ham, and prawns to rice, continue stirring until thoroughly cooked. Cool. Serve mayonnaise separately if desired.

Crab Sunshine Salad

Gwen Marshall
Australia

Salad:

1	large lettuce head
1	pound cooked crabmeat
1	large pawpaw, or rockmelon (substitute cantelope or honeydew and a papaya if preferred)
4	hard-boiled eggs, peeled
2	tablespoon snipped chives, or finely chopped shallots (including green tops)

Dressing:

1/2	cup mayonnaise
1/4	cup French dressing
2	teaspoons gherkin, finely chopped
1	tablespoon tomato sauce
	salt
	freshly ground pepper
	sugar

For dressing, combine all ingredients, seasoning to suit your own taste with salt, pepper, and sugar.

For salad, wash and dry the lettuce leaves and shred finely. Make mounds of lettuce on 4 plates, and pile crabmeat in the center. Peel and seed the pawpaw or rockmelon, cut into thin crescents, and arrange around the crab. Separate the whites from the yolks of the eggs. Push the yolks through a sieve, and sprinkle over crab. Chop the whites finely and sprinkle around the lettuce. Scatter snipped chives over all, and serve with dressing.

In our own way, each of us truly can make a difference, one step at a time.

Chow Mein Noodle Salad

Mary Lou Lowry
Missoula, Montana

1/4 cup onion,
finely chopped

1 cup celery

1/4 cup water

1 chicken bouillon cube

1 3-ounce can
chow mein noodles
(reserve 1/2 cup)

1 can cream of
mushroom soup

1 can chunk-style tuna

1 cup cashew nuts, salted

paprika

Cook onion, celery, water, and bouillon for 5 minutes. Mix remaining ingredients lightly; add onion mixture. Bake in a 1 1/2 quart casserole dish at 325 degrees for 25 minutes, making sure not to over bake the mixture. Top with reserved noodles.

Seafood Salad

Lynell Martel
Bozeman, Montana

1 package lemon gelatin

1 cup boiling water

1 can tomato soup

1 cup mayonnaise

1 cup celery,
finely chopped

stuffed olives, chopped
(to taste)

onion, grated (to taste)

1 4 1/2-ounce can
shrimp or crab, or
1 6 1/2-ounce can tuna,
rinsed and drained

Combine gelatin, boiling water, and soup; cool. When cool, add remaining ingredients. Chill.

Daydream Salad

Gwen Marshall
Australia

Fish, potatoes, and apples are the main ingredients in this deliciously different main course salad. Serve sprinkled with chopped shallots.

1 1/2 pounds firm white fish fillets

3 large boiled potatoes, peeled and cubed

2 sticks celery, finely chopped

2 crisp apples, peeled and diced

1 tablespoon lemon juice

1 cup mayonnaise

1 tablespoon sugar

2 teaspoons prepared horseradish

4 shallots, finely chopped

2 tablespoons parsley, finely chopped

salt

freshly ground pepper

extra chopped shallots (for garnish)

Poach fish fillets in lightly salted water until white and opaque - about 6 minutes. Drain, remove skin and bones, and separate into large flakes. Place in a bowl with potatoes. Toss with celery, apples, and lemon juice.

In another bowl, combine mayonnaise, sugar, horseradish, shallots, parsley, and salt and pepper to taste. Add to fish mixture, toss to combine, and chill until serving time.

Serves 6

Crab Louis

Jane Quinn
Bozeman, Montana

This recipe came from an old Better Homes and Garden Salad Cookbook.

Salad:

- 12   large ripe olives (optional)
- 1   large head lettuce
- 2-3   cups cooked crabmeat, or 2 6 1/2-ounce cans, chilled
- 2   large tomatoes
- 2   hard cooked eggs
- 2   cups celery, chopped

Dressing:

- 1   cup mayonnaise
- 1/4   cup heavy cream, whipped
- 1/4   cup chili sauce
- 1/4   cup green pepper, chopped
- 1/4   cup green onion, chopped (with tops)
- 1   teaspoon lemon juice

Combine dressing ingredients and salt to taste. Line 4 large plates with lettuce leaves. Shred remaining lettuce, arrange on lettuce leaves, and add celery. Remove bits of shell from crabmeat. Reserve claw meat, leave remaining meat in chunks, and arrange on top of lettuce. Circle the salad with wedges of tomato, egg, and olive. Sprinkle with salt. Pour 1/4 cup dressing over each salad. Sprinkle with paprika, top with claw meat. Pass remaining dressing.

JELLO
SALADS

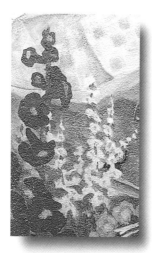

For my birthday, I received a card with this message.....
Remember four simple words:
Live, Love, Laugh, Bloom.
    I stuck that card on my bedroom dresser mirror.
Every morning I read that message and think how
simple it should be to follow that admonition. Summer is
supposed to be a time to spent any way we like. There
should be activities that thrilled us as children. My
days of summer as a child were filled with hikes in the
woods picking gooseberries and mulberries, bicycling all
the way to town to visit my Grandmother, riding my
pony, just exploring, playing "dolls" with baby kittens, caring for the 50 chickens I
was given for my birthday every June, and picnics with neighbors and relatives. To
earn spending money for the big community 4th of July celebration my mother would
put me to work weeding the garden, shucking peas, pitting sour red cherries, picking
raspberries and other such duties.

    I have to say that gardening is not my favorite pursuit but I have learned that
after I get myself positioned , I find that gardening has as much to do with
contemplation as it does about tilling and toiling. It is a way to slow down, so that
you can reconnect with something deeper. It's getting away from the day to day.
Turning things over and being in a quiet place for just a moment or two can bring
peace. Gardening is much like quilting in that you find a place where you are
comfortable and free enough simply to let go.

    Our backyard adventure began in 1984 , when we moved to the country and started to
tame the yard surrounding our century-old farmhouse. The area was completely
overgrown, but we did enjoy the lilac bushes and oriental poppies that had survived decades
of neglect. Gradually we transformed the area - we added walkways, plants, shrubs, new
trees. Now Bill does nearly all the gardening and I reap the harvest . I love using
the fresh vegetables and herbs and especially cutting and arranging flowers from the
garden. He feels strongly about his garden and it's a struggle in the Big Sky
environment! I try to convince him he does not have to do this but.........

Our garden does contain some violas and some hen and chicks which we transplanted to Minnesota from Bill's grandmother's Iowa garden and then moved again when we located to Montana. We come from a long line of "green thumbers." Besides Bill's Grandmother Drummond, there were my Grandmother Bauer and Grandfather Adair. Mostly they grew "down-to-earth" vegetables but their flowers gloriously grew up to the backdoor.

Grandma Bauer was generous with her cut flowers. It was a treat to go home with a bouquet of my own cuttings. And she would share seeds and seedlings but always with the admonition, "Don't say thank you- they won't grow!" Our parents had good luck with sweet corn — no guess as to how many bushels of that were given away.

So you see, gardeners leave their mark on us whether we are gardeners or not. Could you guess — the theme for this summer's activities and classes is flowers and gardens?

In these slowed-down, play-filled days of summer come join us for a class or two. Bring your summer guests. Playtime puts into perspective what happens the rest of the time. Celebrate the season surrounded by friends, children, and grandchildren. Celebrate the season. Take a short retreat to Quilting in the Country.

Play well this summer and remember to Live, Love, Laugh and Bloom.

Jane

Seven Layer Jello

Karalee Mulkey
Broadus, Montana

Don't be intimidated by the list of hints following this recipe, Karalee just wants to pass on what she has learned to make this salad even easier!

6 packages *Knox* gelatin
1 3-ounce package strawberry gelatin
1 can sweetened condensed milk
1 3-ounce package lime gelatin
1 3-ounce package lemon gelatin
1 3-ounce package orange gelatin
1 1/2 cups tap water, divided
4 1/2 cups hot water, divided

Step 1:
Dissolve one package *Knox* gelatin in 1/4 cup tap water. Add the strawberry gelatin and 3/4 cup hot water. Stir until both gelatins are completely dissolved. Pour into a 9 X 13 inch pan sprayed lightly with cooking spray and refrigerate for 20 minutes (perhaps a few minutes longer in the summer).

Step 2:
Dissolve two packages *Knox* gelatin in 1/2 cup water. To this, add sweetened condensed milk and 1 1/2 cups hot water. Stir until gelatin dissolves completely. Pour 1/3 of this mixture (approximately a little more than a cup) over the strawberry gelatin and refrigerate 20 minutes (perhaps a few minutes longer in the summer).

Step 3:
Repeat steps 1 and 2 with lime, lemon, and orange gelatin. The sweetened condensed milk is enough for three layers.

Continued on the next page.

Hints:
Level your pan as best you can in your refrigerator. It is important to make the first layer as level as possible. (Put a paper towel under the low end.) If, despite your efforts, you find that the pan is uneven after it has gelled, put the pan in the microwave for a short period of time (approximately 30 seconds); the gelatin will dissolve enough so that you can reposition it in the refrigerator. When the first layer is level, leave the pan in the refrigerator and pour the succeeding layers in while the pan is still in the refrigerator. This should give you even, level layers.

If the milk layer begins to gel before needed, put it in the microwave for approximately 20 seconds to dissolve it. (Mix this layer in a plastic, microwave-safe measuring cup.) After you add a layer, mix up the next layer so that it can start cooling. You are less likely to have layers dissolve and "bleed" into each other if the layers are somewhat cooled when added to the pan.

At Christmas-time, the following sequences of gelatin - orange, lemon, lime, and strawberry - are a festive combination. You can experiment with the many flavors of gelatin and come up with your own favorite combinations for different holidays. (For instance, layer red, white, and blue for the Fourth of July using cherry and blueberry gelatin.)

Molded Salad

Eva Veltkamp
Bozeman, Montana

1	package lime gelatin
1	package lemon gelatin
2	cups hot water
1	can crushed pineapple and juice
1	cup mayonnaise
1	cup cottage cheese
1	cup canned milk
1	cup chopped nuts
2	teaspoons horseradish

Dissolve lime and lemon gelatin in 2 cups hot water. Cool. Mix remaining ingredients together thoroughly and add to gelatin. Beat with wire whisk until it mixes well. Pour into an oiled mold.

Corny Salad Mold

Jane Quinn
Bozeman, Montana

My Iowa roots originally drew me to this recipe. It seems to be a unique addition to all salad buffets.

2	cups water
1/4	cup cider vinegar
2	tablespoons Dijon mustard
2	3-ounce packages lemon gelatin
1/2	cup red bell pepper, chopped
1/2	cup green bell pepper, chopped
1/2	cup green onions, chopped
1	15 1/4-ounce can whole kernel corn, drained
	vegetable cooking spray
	lettuce leaves (optional)

Combine first 3 ingredients in a small saucepan. Stir well. Sprinkle the gelatin over the vinegar mixture and let stand 1 minute. Cook over low heat until the gelatin is completely dissolved. Pour mixture into a bowl. Cover and chill 1 1/2 hours or until the consistency of unbeaten egg white. Fold in bell peppers, green onions and corn. Spray an 8 inch square baking dish with vegetable spray. Spoon in the gelatin mixture. Cover and chill until firm. This salad looks pretty served on lettuce-lined plates.

Serves 9

Cool Whip Salad

Jo Whiteaker
Bozeman, Montana

2	8-ounce cartons *Cool Whip* topping
1	small box raspberry gelatin
1	can crushed pineapple, drained
1	quart cottage cheese

Mix *Cool Whip* and dry gelatin. Add drained pineapple and cottage cheese, mix and chill. (Any color gelatin works well for this salad and a can of pineapple tidbits are also a nice addition.)

Lemon Crème Salad

Lois Wambolt
Bozeman, Montana

When our Redwork Circle met for a salad potluck, this salad from Lois made a wonderful addition to the amazing array of salads. Lois tried this recipe from a Whitehall, Wisconsin church cookbook, which was a gift from her neighbor and fellow quilter, Joan Johnson.

1	3-ounce package lemon gelatin
1/3	cup sugar
1	cup boiling water
6	ounces frozen lemonade, thawed
1	8-ounce container whipped topping

Combine gelatin and sugar. Add water. Stir in lemonade. Chill until partially set. Fold in whipped topping. Chill until set.

Orange Buttermilk Salad

Juli Rognlie
Bozeman, Montana

Juli was thrilled to discover that her young, finicky daughters would eat this salad. Little do they know that they are eating pineapple!

1	20-ounce can crushed pineapple, undrained
1	6-ounce package orange gelatin
2	cups buttermilk
1	8-ounce carton *Cool Whip* topping, thawed

In a saucepan, bring the pineapple to a boil. Remove from heat and add gelatin. Stir until dissolved. Add buttermilk and mix well. Cool to room temperature. Fold in *Cool Whip*. Pour into a 9 x 9 inch pan. Refrigerate overnight. Cut into squares to serve.

Lemon Salad

Hazel Rafferty, "Quilt-A-Way"
Great Falls, Montana

1	package lemon gelatin
1	cup hot water
3	tablespoons sugar
1	lemon, juice only
3/4	cup cheddar cheese, grated
1	small jar pimentos
1	cup crushed pineapple, drained
	pinch of salt
1	cup whipped cream

Dissolve gelatin in water; let boil 3 minutes. Add sugar and lemon juice. Cool. Add cheese, pimentos, pineapple, and salt; let set until partially firm. Add whipped cream and let set.

Mint Salad

Judy Strohmeyer
Bozeman, Montana

The "mint" in this salad is not what you might expect!

1	package lime gelatin, dry
2	20-ounce cans crushed pineapple, drained
1	package miniature marshmallows
1	pint whipped cream or *Cool Whip*
1	package *Kraft* butter-mints, crushed
	dry roasted peanuts

Mix gelatin, pineapple, and marshmallows together and let stand overnight in refrigerator. Add remaining ingredients, mix and freeze. Remove salad from freezer 15 minutes before serving.

Grandma's Yellow Holiday Salad

Barb Dena
Parachute, Colorado

This is Barb's family recipe for Jello salad. Barb adds chopped nuts, but says that anyone who knew her grandmother will understand when she says that they did not agree on this point! Since Grandma invented the recipe, Barb says she should probably not take liberties with the ingredients.

1   6-ounce box lemon gelatin

1   20-ounce can crushed pineapple, drained

1   small carton cottage cheese

1   8-ounce package cream cheese

1/4   cup *Miracle Whip* salad dressing (optional)

walnut pieces (optional)

Use 1/2 the hot water called for on the package to dissolve the gelatin in this recipe. Blend all ingredients in a blender, adding very well-drained pineapple, cottage cheese, and cream cheese in that order. Barb's grandma always liked to put a good plop of *Miracle Whip* salad dressing in her mixture, but this is optional. Blend the mixture until smooth and pour into a buttered 8 X 8 inch pan, adding the walnut pieces last. Let set until firm. If the salad does not set up firmly, the pineapple was not drained well enough. If it is too firm, it needed a little more pineapple juice.

Our life is frittered away by detail. Simplify, simplify, simplify.
Henry David Thoreau, Walden 1854

Pineapple-Banana Salad

Eleanor Christian
Bozeman, Montana

Salad:

- 2 packages lemon gelatin
- 4 cups boiling water
- 16 large marshmallows, or 2 cups small marshmallows
- 1 20-ounce can crushed pineapple, drained with juice reserved
- 4 bananas, slash down crosswise and thinly slice

Topping:

- 1/2 cup sugar
- 2 tablespoons flour
- 2 eggs, slightly beaten
- 1 cup pineapple juice
- 1 teaspoon lemon juice
- 2 tablespoons butter
- 1 cup whipping cream, whipped

Dissolve gelatin in the boiling water. Add marshmallows and stir until dissolved. Add pineapple and bananas. Cool. Pour into a 9 X 13 inch pan and chill. Cook all topping ingredients except whipping cream in a double boiler over hot water until the mixture is thick like pudding. Cool, then add whipped cream. Spread on top of cold gelatin mixture.

Yum-Yum Ribbon Salad

Jane Quinn
Bozeman, Montana

This recipe came to my mother, Maxine, from my aunt Fern Bauer. It has been a part of our Christmas Eve Supper for at least 55 years. That is tradition at it's best! (I have altered the colors of the top and bottom layers of gelatin to reflect seasonal themes.)

1	package red gelatin
1	package lemon gelatin
1	dozen large marshmallows, snipped
1	3-ounce package cream cheese
1	cup salad dressing
1	small can crushed pineapple, undrained
1	cup heavy cream, whipped
1	package green gelatin
	lettuce leaves

Dissolve red gelatin according to package directions. Pour into a 9 x 13 inch glass dish. Cool to set.

Dissolve lemon gelatin. Add marshmallows. Stir or whip until marshmallows are dissolved. Whip in softened cream cheese and salad dressing. Add pineapple and fold in whipped cream. Pour over red gelatin and return to refrigerator. Dissolve green gelatin and let cool until consistency of egg white. Pour over lemon layer. Return to refrigerator. Cut into squares and serve on lettuce leaves.

Strawberry-Rhubarb Spring Salad

Mary Ellen Woolley
Bozeman, Montana

Everyone loves being on a committee with Mary Ellen. She has great recipes and ideas. I don't think she's ever made anything that wasn't out-of-this-world!

6 cups rhubarb (about 1 1/2-pounds), trimmed and cut in 1/2-inch slices or smaller

1 1/4 cups sugar

3/4 cups water

2 envelopes (1 tablespoon each) unflavored gelatin

2 tablespoons lemon juice

1 3-ounce package strawberry gelatin (using 1 cup hot water and 3/4 cup cold water)

1 pint (or more) fresh strawberries, stemmed and sliced

halved strawberries, for garnish

In a large saucepan, mix the rhubarb, sugar, and 1/2 cup of the water. Bring mixture to a boil over medium heat; reduce the heat and simmer about 10 minutes, stirring occasionally until the rhubarb is tender. Meanwhile, soften the gelatin in the remaining 1/4 cup water and lemon juice. Stir the gelatin mixture into the hot rhubarb to dissolve the gelatin. Add the strawberry gelatin with the water to the rhubarb mixture. Chill the mixture until slightly thickened. Fold in the sliced strawberries. Pour into a mold or use a *Pyrex* dish, and chill until firm.

Orange-Apricot Salad

Rose McCaig
Pointe Claire, Quebec, Canada

Salad:

1	15-ounce can apricots
1	20-ounce can crushed pineapple
1	6-ounce package orange gelatin
2	cups hot water
1	cup reserved fruit juice
1	cup miniature marshmallows

Topping:

1/2	cup sugar
3/4	cup reserved fruit juice
1	egg, well beaten
2	tablespoons cornstarch
1/4	cup reserved fruit juice
2	tablespoons butter
1	cup whipping cream, whipped
3/4	cup cheddar cheese, grated

For salad, drain apricots and pineapple, reserving juice. Dissolve gelatin in hot water. Add 1 cup of reserved fruit juice, apricots, and pineapple. When partially set, add marshmallows and pour into mold. Chill until set.

For topping, combine sugar and 3/4 cup of reserved fruit juice. Bring to a boil. Add hot syrup to beaten egg, gradually combining cornstarch and remaining 1/4 cup juice. Cook over low heat until thick. Add butter. Cool. Add whipped cream. Spread over gelatin. Sprinkle with grated cheese.

8 servings

Every ending leads to a new beginning, a bright window of opportunity, and more reasons to celebrate.

Orange Salad Supreme

Diane Donnelly
Bozeman, Montana

This salad is a long-time favorite of Diane's family. The recipe originally came from her aunt, Verta Reeves, of Gordon, Nebraska. Verta made one quilt in her lifetime, an "album patch" design out of 30's and 40's fabrics, which Diane is proud to own. Diane takes time away from her "real" job to work some Saturdays and proof the newsletter at Quilting in the Country. She is a precious friend.

1	3-ounce package tapioca pudding
1	3-ounce package instant vanilla pudding
1	3-ounce package orange gelatin
2	cups hot water
2	cups *Cool Whip* topping
1	11-ounce can mandarin oranges

Mix both flavors of pudding, gelatin, and water together and cook until thick and bubbly, being careful to not scald the mixture. Cool completely. Add the *Cool Whip* and mandarin oranges. Chill.

Variations:
Use lemon gelatin and pineapple chunks for a different taste!

Orange Salad

Jo Whiteaker
Bozeman, Montana

I admire Jo's quiet, unassuming manner. Her award-winning quilts are impeccable.

1	11-ounce can mandarin oranges
1	3-ounce package orange gelatin
1	pint orange sherbet
1	banana

Drain the juice from the mandarin oranges into a cup and add enough water to make 1 cup. Heat juice to a boil and add to the gelatin while still hot. Add sherbet and gently mix with an egg beater until smooth. Chill until almost set; add oranges and sliced banana. Chill until firm.

Apricot Cheese Delight Salad

Cydell Chambers
Bozeman, Montana

This recipe can be divided in half easily. Try this recipe when you're doing an array of salads.

Salad:

1	29-ounce can apricots, drained and chopped (reserve juice)
1	29-ounce can crushed pineapple, drained (reserve juice)
2	6-ounce packages orange gelatin
2	cups hot water
1	cup reserved fruit juice

Topping:

1/2	cup sugar
3	tablespoons flour, rounded
1	egg, slightly beaten
1	cup reserved fruit juice
2	tablespoons butter
1	cup whipping cream, whipped
3/4	cup cheddar cheese, grated

Dissolve gelatin in hot water. Add fruit juice to the water and gelatin. Then add the apricots and pineapple while you stir evenly. Chill until firm.

Combine the sugar and flour. Blend in egg. Slowly stir in juice. Cook over low heat, stirring constantly until thickened. Stir in butter and cool. Fold in cream and spread over the chilled gelatin. Sprinkle with cheese.

A friend is a gift
you give yourself.
Robert Louis Stevenson

Stained Glass Salad

Kimberli Hart McCullough
Big Timber, Montana

This is a colorful salad and slightly sweet due to the crust. Kimberli's three active boys always request it for their cub scouts, church, and sporting event potlucks. It can be made a day ahead to suit a quilter's busy schedule. It is truly easy and a nice change for variety.

Mixture Number One

- 1 package each of three different gelatin flavors (Kimberli likes blueberry, orange, and raspberry)
- 1 1/2 cups hot water for each package

Mixture Number Two

- 2 envelopes unflavored gelatin
- 1 cup pineapple juice

Mixture Number Three

- 2 cups heavy whipping cream
- 1/2 cup sugar
- 1 teaspoon vanilla

Crust Mixture

- 2 dozen graham crackers, or vanilla wafers
- 1/2 cup softened butter
- 1/2 cup granulated sugar

Directions continued on the next page.

Mixture Number One:
Mix each flavor in a separate bowl and pour into 3 separate pans. (Use bread/loaf pans for a thicker setting.) When set; cut into1/2 inch squares.

Mixture Number Two:
Dissolve gelatin in 1/4 cup cold water. Add hot pineapple juice. Let cool until just starting to set.

Mixture Number Three:
Whip cream adding sugar & vanilla

Crust:
Cut mixture together with a fork. Press 2/3 of crust mixture into 9 X 13 pan.

Fold mixture Number Two into Mixture Number Three. Then fold cubes of gelatin (Mixture Number One) in carefully. Spoon into a 9 x 13 inch pan which has been lined with two thirds of the crust mixture (recipe follows). Dispense remaining crust crumbles over the top of the stained glass salad. Refrigerate at least 8-12 hours. Cut into squares and serve on a bed of lettuce.

Blueberry Salad

Cydell Chambers
Bozeman, Montana

Cydell submitted this recipe from my good friend, Jane Edie, who passed away in 1986. I miss Jane.

2	3.4-ounce packages raspberry gelatin
2	cups boiling water
1	cup sour cream
1	15-ounce can crushed pineapple with juice
1	tablespoon lemon juice
1	can blueberry pie filling

Dissolve gelatin in water and cool. Add the sour cream, pineapple, lemon juice, and blueberry pie filling, stirring evenly. Chill until firm. Makes 12 small gelatin molds or a 9 x 13 inch container.

Rhode Island Red Top Salad

Diane and Gary Arganbright - "The Quilting Hen and Antiques"
Carter, Montana

This recipe came from Diane Arganbright's grandmother, Marie Elizabeth Landenberger, who also raised Standard Single Comb Rhode Island Red Chickens. The recipe was given to her in 1968.

1 package cherry gelatin
2 3/4 cup boiling water, divided
1/2 pound marshmallows
1 package lime gelatin
1 8-ounce package cream cheese
  dash of salt
1/2 cup mayonnaise
1 cup celery, minced
1/2 cup nuts, chopped
1 medium can crushed pineapple, drained
1 cup whipping cream, whipped

For bottom of mold, dissolve cherry gelatin in 1 3/4 cups boiling water. Put aside to set. Dissolve marshmallows and lime gelatin in 1 cup boiling water. Stir until marshmallows are dissolved. Cool. Beat cream cheese, salt and mayonnaise with an electric beater until light and fluffy. Stir in celery, nuts, and pineapple. Add marshmallow mixture. Fold in whipped cream. Pour over the red gelatin. Chill and set.

Buttermilk Salad

Eva Veltkamp
Bozeman, Montana

1 1/2 cups orange juice
4 tablespoons honey
1 cup buttermilk
1 envelope unflavored gelatin
  fresh strawberries, peaches or cantelope, to taste

Bring orange juice and honey to a boil. Put buttermilk in blender. Sprinkle gelatin on top and allow mixture to soften. Whirl. When soft, combine orange juice and buttermilk mixture and cool until thick. Add fruit and pour into jello mold.

Rainbow Jello

Jan Rutledge
Bozeman, Montana

This is so pretty and tasty.

Clear Layers:

4   3-ounce packages flavored gelatin

3   cups hot water, divided

3   cups cold water, divided

Milk Layers:

3   3-ounce packages gelatin

2 1/4 cups hot water, divided

2 1/2 cups evaporated milk, divided

Jello Layers:

1. Black Cherry - Clear
2. Cherry - Milk
3. Lime - Clear
4. Lemon - Milk
5. Orange - Clear
6. Orange - Milk
7. Strawberry - Clear

    lettuce leaves (optional)

Step 1:
Mix one package of flavored gelatin according to directions using 3/4 cup each of hot and cold water. Pour into glass 9 X 13 pan. Refrigerate until firm.

Step 2:
Mix one package of flavored gelatin according to directions using 3/4 cup of hot water and 1/2 cup evaporated milk. When cool, pour mixture onto first layer. Refrigerate until firm.

Step 3:
Repeat steps 1 & 2 twice, using different flavors if desired.

Step 4:
Repeat step 1 with final flavor. Pour final layer on top.

Cut into squares and serve individually on a lettuce leaf, or cut into small squares and place them all in a clear glass salad bowl to serve.

Orange Sherbet Salad

Juli Rognlie
Bozeman, Montana

This salad recipe comes from Juli's grandmother. It is the inspiration behind her beautiful pineapple/orange challenge block.

1	6-ounce package orange gelatin
2	cups boiling water
1	pint orange sherbet
1	11-ounce can mandarin oranges
1	20-ounce can crushed pineapple, drained

Dissolve gelatin in boiling water. Add sherbet and allow to melt. Add fruit. Pour into a 9 x 9 inch pan. Chill.

Red Raspberry Molded Salad

Jane Quinn
Bozeman, Montana

1	6-ounce package raspberry gelatin
1	cup boiling water
1	3-ounce package cream cheese
1	box frozen red raspberries, sweetened
1/4	cup ground nuts

Dissolve gelatin in boiling water and add frozen berries. Stir until berries have thawed. Let chill until mixture begins to thicken. While the gelatin is chilling, make cream cheese balls and roll them in ground nuts, pressing hard enough to make sure the nuts cling to the cheese. Arrange the balls in the bottom of a ring mold. Pour gelatin over them and place the mold in the refrigerator to become firm.

Lime Pear Salad

Nancy K. Hall, "Quilt-A-Way"
Great Falls, Montana

1	large box lime gelatin
1	cup hot pear juice, reserved
2	tablespoons cream
1	8-ounce package cream cheese
1	16-ounce can pears, mashed, reserve juice
1	cup whipping cream, whipped

Dissolve gelatin with hot pear juice. Add two tablespoons cream to the cream cheese. Mix together to soften the cream cheese. Stir the softened cream cheese into the gelatin mixture. Mash one pint of pears and add to the gelatin cream cheese mixture. Stir one cup whipped cream into the above mixture. Pour into a mold if desired and let stand overnight before serving.

Pretzel Salad

Sandi Atkinson
Ritzville, Washington

We loved it when Sandi made an impromptu visit in a Quilting in the Country class one summer. Her recipe is fun as a salad or as a dessert.

Salad:

2 1/2 cups pretzels, crushed

3/4 cup margarine, melted

3 tablespoons sugar

1 8-ounce package cream cheese

1 cup sugar

1 envelope *Dream Whip* topping

Topping:

1 6-ounce package strawberry gelatin

2 cups boiling water

2 10-ounce packages frozen sliced strawberries

Mix pretzels, margarine, and sugar and spread in a 9 X 13 inch pan. Bake at 375 degrees for 10 minutes. Set aside and cool. Mix cream cheese and sugar thoroughly. Mix *Dream Whip* according to directions on the box; fold into cream cheese mixture.

Dissolve gelatin thoroughly in hot water. Add frozen berries to gelatin until berries are thawed and gelatin starts to set. Pour mixture over cream cheese layer. Refrigerate for a few hours before serving.

Serves 8-12

Americans like gelatin. More than 1,134,239 packages of Jell-O gelatin are purchased or eaten every day. The 413 million packages of Jell-O produced each year would stretch three-fifths of the way around the world if stacked end-to-end.
— Bozeman Daily Chronicle

Raspberry Pretzel Salad

Shirley Drake Naismith
Grand Forks, North Dakota

1	6-ounce package raspberry gelatin
2	10-ounce packages frozen raspberries
1	4-ounce package cream cheese
1/4	cup powdered sugar
1/2	small tub *Cool Whip* topping
1 1/2	cups pretzel sticks, crushed
3/4	cup melted butter

Dissolve gelatin in 2 cups hot water. Add raspberries until thawed. Place in a pretty glass serving bowl and let set. Cream cream cheese and powdered sugar. Fold in *Cool Whip*. Spread on top of gelatin. Refrigerate. Mix sugar, melted butter, and pretzels. Bake in a 9 x 13 inch pan for 10 minutes at 350 degrees. Cool. Break up mix. Sprinkle on top of cream layer.

Jellied Spring Salad

Marian Neill
Whitehall, Montana

1	tablespoon *Knox* gelatin
1/4	cup cold water
1 1/2	cups hot water
1	tablespoon lemon juice
1	tablespoon vinegar
1	teaspoon salt
1	cup cucumber, diced
1/2	cup green onions, sliced
1/2	cup radishes, sliced
1	cup celery, chopped

Soften gelatin in cold water; dissolve in hot water. Add lemon juice, vinegar, and salt. Chill until partially set, add remaining ingredients. Chill until firm in an oiled mold. Serve on crisp lettuce with mayonnaise.

Lemon Cream Cheese Salad

Shirley Johnson, "Quilt-A-Way"
Great Falls, Montana

This recipe was handed down to Shirley from a special aunt, and is over 100 years old. Shirley says it is always a favorite for Easter dinner; simple to make and simply delicious to eat!

1 cup crushed pineapple, drained (juice reserved)

1 package lemon gelatin

1 cup *Best Food* mayonnaise

1 cup regular cream cheese

20 marshmallows, cut in quarters

1/2 pint whipping cream, whipped

Use pineapple juice with water to make 2 cups liquid for gelatin. Mix mayonnaise and cream cheese to a smooth paste and add to cool gelatin. Add drained pineapple and marshmallows (whole marshmallows soften better than miniatures). Fold in whipped cream and mix carefully.

Ice Cream Salad

Edith Martin
Exira, Iowa

1 package orange gelatin

1 cup boiling water

1 pint ice cream

1 8-ounce can crushed pineapple

1 2-ounce package nuts, crushed

cookie crumbs for crust (optional)

Dissolve gelatin in water. Add ice cream, pineapple, and nuts. Pour into a mold and refrigerate.

Holiday Nog Jello Salad

Juli Rognlie
Bozeman, Montana

2	cups boiling water
1	6-ounce package lemon gelatin
1/2	cup cold water
1 1/2	cups cold milk
1	3-ounce package vanilla instant pudding mix
2	teaspoons rum flavoring extract
1/2	teaspoon ground nutmeg
2	cups thawed *Cool Whip* topping

Stir boiling water into gelatin in a large bowl until dissolved; stir in cold water. Cool to room temperature. Pour milk into a medium-size bowl. Add pudding mix. Beat with a wire whisk about one minute. Stir pudding into cooled gelatin until smooth. Stir in rum extract and nutmeg, refrigerate for approximately 1 hour until slightly thickened. Gently stir in *Cool Whip* with a whisk until smooth and creamy. Pour into a mold. Refrigerate 4 hours until firm. Unmold onto plate.

Lime Gelatin Salad

Mary Ellen Woolley
Bozeman, Montana

1	small can crushed pineapple
1	3-ounce package lime gelatin
12	marshmallows
1/2	pint creamed cottage cheese
1/2	cup chopped walnuts (optional)
1/2	pint whipping cream, with added sugar below
1/3	cup sugar (less - 1 or 2 tablespoons sugar)

Drain juice from pineapple and add enough water to make two cups. Bring pineapple mixture almost to a boil and add gelatin and marshmallows. Let dissolve and remove from heat; cool until slightly firm. Add cottage cheese, pineapple, nuts, and mix together. Fold in sweetened whipping cream. Pour into a large mold or individual molds and chill. (A flat glass baking dish also works well).

Blueberry Jello Salad

Sue Broyles
Rapelje, Montana

Even Sue's teenagers like this gelatin salad. It is great for potlucks because it is fast and serves many.

Salad:

1   6-ounce package blackberry gelatin

2   cups boiling water

1   20-ounce can crushed pineapple, undrained

1   21-ounce can blueberry pie filling

Topping:

1   8-ounce package cream cheese

1/2 cup sour cream

1/2 cup sugar

1   teaspoon vanilla

1/2 cup chopped pecans or walnuts

Dissolve gelatin in boiling water. Add the pineapple - juice and all - and pie filling. Pour into a glass 9" x 13" pan. Mix topping ingredients and when set, spread the topping over the gelatin. Sprinkle nuts on top. You may substitute cherry gelatin and cherry pie filling for the blackberry gelatin and blueberry pie filling.

20 servings

LEGUME
SALADS

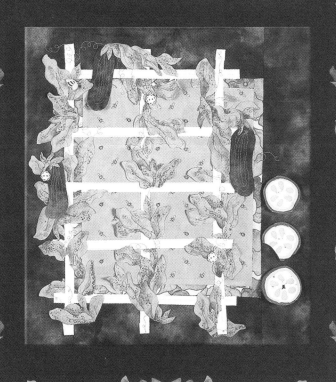

As far back as I can remember, my Mother's hands were busy making "pretty things". In the early 40's, we were dirt poor farmers or poor dirt farmers - I'm not sure which! Mom always worked a "town job", not because she wanted to, but because she had to. But no matter how tired or how busy, she always found a few minutes to sew or do "fancy work". I remember well the little dresses my sisters and I wore to school; little dresses made from the printed cotton sacks that arrived at our farm full of chicken feed. Embellished with bits of lace and embroidery, we didn't know they weren't from the Montgomery Ward catalog. As each of her four children was born, she stitched a quilt; each filled with much love. Upon the completion of three of the quilt tops, they were carefully wrapped and put away. One might think that each daughter would receive her quilt upon her marriage, but such was not the case. Maybe she was waiting to make sure the marriages lasted - they did! When my sisters and I were in our late twenties or early thirties, Mom got out the quilt tops and began to quilt them. It took a long time; her fingers had become stiff with rheumatoid arthritis. She wore no protective thimble and her fingers would eventually become so pricked and sore that they would bleed. The quilt would be laid aside for a few weeks until her fingers healed and then she would quilt some more. It was always a mystery to me why she didn't protect the left-hand finger, since while doing any fine hand stitching on a garment or embroidery work she always wore a thimble on her right hand finger. By the time she had quilted both my younger and older sisters' quilts, she had become somewhat distressed because her quilting stitches were not as small and even, not as precise as they had once been. So my beautiful Grandmother's Flower Garden quilt that had been pieced in 1938 and 1939 was not to be quilted by Mother. In the mid-70's, the quilt was sent to Alma Shimmins who lives in Paradise Valley south of Livingston to be quilted. Alma did a beautiful job. It is one of the great regrets of my life that I did not chart the quilt. At one time Mom would tell me: "The little blue print was a dress I made for Ruthie" and "The orange and brown flowered piece was one of Grandma Burnett's aprons" - she knew them all. When I realized how important that information was to me, she could no longer remember. My sisters' quilts were the last two quilts Mom quilted. She was then in her mid 60's.

Born Ruby E. Amanda Wight, Mother was the granddaughter of Montana pioneers James Madison Wight and Maryann Ettien Wight. The extended Wight family came into the Pig Eye Basin near Judith Gap in 1884 with members of the Ettien family including Jim Ettien, the documented discoverer of the Yogo Sapphire Mine. Many descendents of "Grandpa Matt and Grandma Maryann" still live in Montana - the Duffield's, Higham's, and Tuggle's from south of Billings, and the Taylor and Mitchell families of the Livingston area.

Mother's stitching expertise was self-taught for the most part. She was extremely precise and had a wonderful sense of color. She passed away in 1993 and left a beautiful legacy of quilts, quilted pillows; crocheted work - pillows, wallhangings, tablecloths, bedspreads, doilies and dresser sets, baby layettes, mittens and caps, afghans, bed linens - the list goes on; tatted edgings on towels and handkerchiefs, delicately embroidered pillowcases and many, many more "pretty things". Her most cherished legacy, however, was teaching her 3 daughters and 4 grandchildren the love, appreciation, and enjoyment of beautiful "fancy work".

Glenda Mitchell
Livingston, Montana

Glenda's Heart of Paradise Salad recipe and challenge block are featured in this book (see Green Salads). She is a talented quilt maker and continues her mother's legacy.

Spicy Black Bean Salad

Coco Beland
Bozeman, Montana

Yummy!

Salad:

1 1/2 cups dried black beans, soaked and cooked al dente

1/2 cup carrot, blanched and diced

1/2 cup celery, blanched and diced

fresh cilantro, chopped

Dressing:

1/4 cup light olive oil

3 tablespoons fresh lime juice

1 1/2 teaspoons fresh lime zest

1 garlic clove, minced

2 tablespoons white wine vinegar

3 pinches cayenne pepper

1 or 2 jalapeno peppers, seeded and diced

Mix together dressing ingredients. Toss with beans, celery, and carrots. Marinate 1/2 hour. Garnish with fresh chopped cilantro.

Evie's Calico Bean Salad

Pat Walter
Pine Island, Minnesota

Pat is an e-mail buddy. She's full of helpful hints.

Salad:

- 1   15-ounce can black-eyed peas, drained
- 1   15-ounce can pinto beans
- 1   small jar pimento
- 1   small onion, chopped
- 1   cup celery, chopped
- 1   cup green pepper, chopped
- 1   15-ounce can white shoe peg corn

Dressing:

- 3/4   cup cider vinegar
- 1/2   cup oil
- 1   cup sugar
- 1   teaspoon salt
- 1/2   teaspoon pepper
- 1   tablespoon water

Mix dressing ingredients and boil. Cool. Pour over salad ingredients. Let marinate. Drain well before serving.

Italian Bean Salad

Beryl Littlefield, "Quilt-A-Way"
Great Falls, Montana

This is a salad that Beryl eats often at a small Italian restaurant in
Boise, Idaho.

3   celery stalks

1   red onion, chopped

1   sweet red pepper

1   green bell pepper

1   yellow pepper

2   large tomatoes

1   15-ounce can garbanzo beans, drained

1   15-ounce can red kidney beans, drained

1   2-ounce can sliced ripe olives, drained

1   cup green salad olives (juice reserved)

1   6 1/2-ounce jar marinated artichoke hearts, drained (oil reserved)

2   cloves garlic, minced

1   teaspoon ground thyme

2   teaspoons ground oregano

Chop all vegetables and place them in a large bowl with beans, drained olives and artichoke hearts. Mix together the reserved artichoke oil with about 1/3 cup vinegar solution from the green olives; add garlic, thyme and oregano and pour dressing over the salad. Mix, cover, and refrigerate. This salad tastes even better the second day.

Open your eyes.

Look.

Vegetable Bean Salad

Marian Neill
Whitehall, Montana

When you see Marian's name on our class schedule, try to attend one of her classes. A special time will be in store.

Salad:

2   15-ounce cans French-style green beans

1   small can *LeSeuer* tiny peas

1   15-ounce can shoe peg corn

1   cup celery, finely chopped

1   cup green pepper, finely chopped

1/2 cup onion, minced

1   small jar pimento, diced

Dressing:

1 1/4 cups sugar

1/2 cup salad oil

3/4 cup vinegar

1   tablespoon water

1   teaspoon salt

    pepper

Boil dressing ingredients for 5 minutes, cool. Pour dressing over vegetables; cover and refrigerate for several hours before serving. This salad keeps well in the refrigerator.

Marinated Bean Salad

Bunny Haines
Missoula, Montana

Doll-making is Bunny's first love, but she's enthusiastic about quilting, too.

1   16-ounce can great
     Northern beans,
     rinsed and drained

1   15-ounce can
     black beans,
     rinsed and drained

1   15-ounce can
     kidney beans,
     rinsed and drained

1   8 3/4-ounce can
     whole kernel corn,
     rinsed and drained

4   green onions, sliced

1   carrot, chopped

1/2 cup *Real Lemon* lemon
     juice from concentrate

1/3 cup olive oil

1   garlic clove, pressed

1/2 teaspoon salt

1/2 teaspoon pepper

1   teaspoon chili powder
     lettuce (optional)
     tomato (optional)

Combine first 6 ingredients. Stir together juice and next 5 ingredients; toss with bean mixture. Cover and chill for 2 hours or up to 4 days. Serve with lettuce and tomato, if desired.

*To accomplish great things,
we must not only act,
but also dream, not only plan,
but also believe.
Anatole France*

Black Bean and Barley Salsa Salad

Juli Rognlie
Bozeman, Montana

Juli and her family like to serve this salad with hamburgers.

2	cups water
1	cup quick-cooking barley
1	cup corn
1	cup tomato, chopped
1/2	cup fresh cilantro, chopped
1/3	cup red bell pepper, chopped
1/4	cup red onion, chopped
1/4	cup green onion, chopped
1	can black beans, rinsed
1/4	cup lemon juice
1	teaspoon hot pepper sauce
1	teaspoon olive oil
1/4	teaspoon cumin
1/4	teaspoon pepper

Cook barley in the water. Add corn to barley during the final 2 minutes of cooking time. Chill. Add remaining ingredients.

Crunchy Green Pea Salad

Patti's Bernina
Sunburst, Montana

1	10-ounce package frozen peas (thaw with water to remove ice)
1	cup celery, chopped
1	cup cauliflower or broccoli, chopped
2	tablespoons pimento, chopped
1	cup cashews, macadamia nuts, or sunflower seeds
1/4	cup crisp bacon, chopped
1/2	cup sour cream
1/2	teaspoon Dijon mustard
1	small clove garlic, chopped
1	cup ranch dressing

Mix all ingredients together. Let sit for a while to blend the flavors. Eat and enjoy.

Minted Pea Salad

Juli Rognlie
Bozeman, Montana

This refreshing salad is wonderful on a hot summer day!

1/2	cup mayonnaise
1/4	cup sour cream
1/4	cup fresh mint, minced
1/4	teaspoon Dijon mustard
	dash pepper
3	cups frozen peas, thawed
1	small onion, finely chopped

Toss all ingredients together and chill at least 1 hour before serving. Stir and serve.

Green Pea Salad

Diane Donnelly
Bozeman, Montana

Diane received this recipe from her friend, Becky Vaira, a Montana native and wonderful wife and mother. It's one of Diane's favorite recipes. I remember Diane bringing this recipe to a potluck where there were two salads and ten desserts! Poor planning? - maybe not!

Salad:

1   package frozen green peas, rinsed

   lettuce, chopped

   green onion, chopped

   hard boiled eggs, chopped

   bacon or 'Bacos', cooked, crumbled

   Colby/Cheddar cheese, grated

Dressing:

1/2 + cup mayonnaise

2   teaspoons lemon juice

1/2 + cup sour cream

   basil

   salt and pepper

   celery salt

Mix salad ingredients together, toss with dressing, and chill. This salad tastes even better the second day!

Choose a job you love, and your will never have to work a day in your life.
Confucius

Bean Salad

Elizabeth Abts
Omaha, Nebraska

My sister-in-law, Liz, really is a great cook!

1	red sweet onion
2	green peppers
3	tomatoes
2	cans chili-style beans, drained with juice discarded
1	bottle Catalina salad dressing (8-ounce)
8	ounces cheddar cheese, grated
1	head lettuce, shredded
1/3	bag corn chips, crumbled

Dice onion, peppers, and tomatoes, and add to beans. Add dressing and marinate in refrigerator overnight. Just before serving, add cheese, lettuce, and chips. (The main recipe can be stored in the refrigerator for days on end. Just spoon out and add the lettuce, cheese, and chips before serving.)

Christy's Salad

Marianne Liebmann
Marianne received this recipe from her friend Christy in Minnesota.

Salad:

6-7	slices fried bacon, drained and crumbled
3/4	cup Swiss cheese, shredded
1 1/2	cups tiny frozen peas
1	small red onion, chopped

Dressing:

1	cup real mayonnaise
1/2	cup white sugar
	lettuce, chopped

Combine salad ingredients in a bowl, cover, and store overnight in the refrigerator.

Mix dressing ingredients and store, separate from salad mixture, overnight in the refrigerator. On the day of serving, toss salad and dressing with chopped lettuce.

Crunchy Pea Salad

Terry Pozzi
Carson City, Nevada

Terry adds shrimp or crab to this recipe for an extra touch. She has been making this salad for a long time for quilt guild potlucks and says that everyone seems to like it. Although she lives in Carson City, Nevada, Terry tells that when she was a child, she lived with her parents in Bridger Canyon on the Flaming Arrow Ranch where her father was a caretaker. It truly is a small world!

1	small package frozen peas
2	hard boiled eggs, chopped
1	can water chestnuts, sliced
1	small jar pimentos, chopped
1/3	cup green onions, sliced
1/2	cup celery, sliced
1/3	cup mayonnaise
1	tablespoon hot mustard
1/3	tablespoon garlic, minced, or garlic powder

Combine first 6 ingredients. Mix mayonnaise, mustard, and garlic and add to vegetables. Stir lightly. Cover and chill.

Crisp Bean Salad

Eleanor Christian
Bozeman, Montana

Eleanor's great grandparents were the original homesteaders at our place. It is very special to have photographs and history shared by Eleanor.

Salad:

1	15-ounce can *Del Monte* mixed salad vegetables
1	15-ounce can French-style sliced green beans
1	15-ounce can small green lima beans
1	small jar pimentos, diced
4-6	celery stalks, diced
1	small bunch fresh green onions, finely chopped

Dressing:

1 1/2	cups sugar
1/2	cup salad oil
1	cup vinegar
	dash of garlic salt

Drain the vegetables. Add pimentos, celery, and onion.

Mix the dressing ingredients, stirring until blended.

Let stand overnight or for several hours in the refrigerator.

10 servings

Bean Sprout Salad

Debbie Grabb
Billings, Montana

Debbie loves to hand-finish old quilt tops and save old, treasured quilts. She says she has met the most wonderful people through quilting. I feel the same way!

2	cups fresh bean sprouts
2	medium cucumbers, chopped
1/4	cup soy sauce
2	tablespoons vinegar
1	tablespoon sesame oil
1	teaspoon sugar
1/8	teaspoon dry mustard
	dash Tabasco sauce
1	tablespoon sesame seeds, toasted

Cook sprouts in boiling water for 2 minutes. Drain, chill, and add remaining ingredients. Toss and chill.

Sharon's Crunchy Green Pea Salad

Sharon Davis
Bozeman, Montana, and Dallas, Texas

1	1-pound bag frozen peas
1/4	cup mayonnaise
2	tablespoons Dijon mustard
1 1/2	cups celery, thinly sliced
1/4	cup Spanish-style peanuts (use 1/2 cup if preferred)
	lettuce leaves (optional)

Place peas in a colander and run hot water over them briefly to thaw. Drain well. Mix mayonnaise and mustard. Add the peas, celery, and peanuts and stir gently to blend. Serve in individual lettuce cups, or line a bowl with lettuce leaves and add salad.

Serves 6

Frozen Pea Salad

Lorraine Pratt
Bozeman, Montana

In no time at all, Lorraine has become a talented quiltmaker.

1	head lettuce, chopped	Mix lettuce, onions, water chestnuts, celery, and green peppers together. Spread frozen peas over the top. Mix mayonnaise with sugar and spread over the peas. Let salad set in the refrigerator until the next day. Stir and serve.
	green onions, chopped	
	water chestnuts, chopped	
	celery, sliced small	
	green peppers, diced	
1	package frozen peas	
1	cup mayonnaise	
2	tablespoons sugar	

Bean Salad

Della Berg, "The Plaid Square"
Glasgow, Montana

2	15-ounce cans kidney beans, drained	Stir all ingredients together and serve.
3	sweet pickles, chopped	
1	small onion, chopped	
1/2	teaspoon salt	
4	hard boiled eggs, chopped	
1/4	cup celery, diced	
1/8	teaspoon pepper	
1/4	cup mayonnaise	

PASTA
SALADS

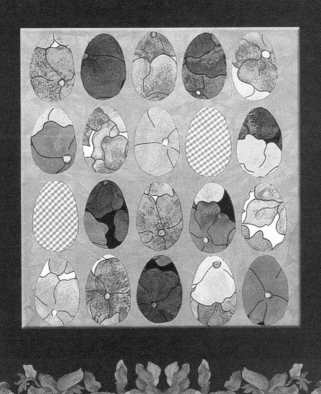

Dear Friends,

I rarely make New Years Resolutions, but I did make a pledge at the beginning of this new millennium and thus far, I have done fairly well abiding by it. Yes, I think that is the correct way to describe my resolution to _have a life_! The demands of wife, mother, grandmother, friend, community member, quilt shop owner were beginning to take their toll. The pace was giving me the feeling that my life was out of control. In my "previous life," as I had become to view it, I had close friends, I did some special things for family and friends, did some entertaining, sang in the church choir, made some special gifts, made some quilts, but now I felt my life was _too busy_...... I had gotten so busy taking care of business that I had forgotten to take care of myself.

When I was young, the adults ("dilts", as my kids called them) told me when to slow down. "Take a nap," they would say, "I think someone is tired." I tried to recollect those carefree feelings of childhood. What I discovered was this: what was desirable then was not so different now in the middle years of my life. I needed to make some small shifts in my life style. A total remodeling was not necessary, but I did need to make some changes. What did I like to do? How about an old hobby? Embroidery or experimenting with a new recipe would be fun. For sure I needed to add some reading and exercise.

So, I pledged to take control of my life. I was going to set priorities instead of just letting one day dissolve into another. I was offering things to my customers that I wanted for myself. They were offered creative outlets for energy and expression, an enjoyable hobby or maybe even a money making adventure, quality time with others during retreats, clubs and classes, an opportunity to relax and enjoy being productive at the same time. How could I give as well as get? How could I incorporate those same opportunities into my own life, while continuing to make them possible for others? I needed to ask myself an honest question: -- whose standards am I living by, anyway? It was important for me to stop long enough to figure out what I really cared about; then, to begin making choices accordingly.

I knew I was just too busy. I needed to set priorities and focus on what was needed. Letting some things go — that was the answer. For instance, I asked myself, would I rather go to my son's "Family and Friends Weekend" sponsored by his company and the 50th wedding anniversary of friends in my hometown in Iowa? (I was the flower girl in their wedding party!) Or would I rather go to this year's "Quilt Market?"

Guess what I chose!

So you ask, what does this have to do with me? I seriously doubt that your life is that much different than mine. Even people in retirement say they are busier than they've ever been. My resolutions are going fairly well, not perfectly, but focused, for the main part. The mild winter has allowed me to walk nearly every day, and the days seem almost magical now. "Having a life" doesn't seem that difficult most days. New natural, positive energy seems abundant as the seasons change. And I feel more rested, more energized, lighter of spirit as I consciously work on my resolutions each day. I'm hopeful that by sharing this, you might find meaningful ways to energize and focus too! Please sit back, relax, and remind yourself how important it is to create some time or some thing special just for you. Taking this time will be a gift to those close to you, as well as to yourself. I hope that you find a "gift" that's just right for you in our summer schedule of fun classes and events!

Til next time,

Jane

Spaghetti Salad

Linda Grossman, "Quilt-A-Way"
Great Falls, Montana

This recipe makes a lot!

1	10-ounce package spaghetti, cooked, drained, and cooled
1	can shrimp, broken
3/4	cup mayonnaise
3/4	cup French dressing
1/2	cup sweet pickle relish
1/2	teaspoon celery salt
1/2	teaspoon garlic salt
1/2	teaspoon onion salt
	tomato, chopped
	celery, chopped
	green pepper, chopped

Mix together all ingredients except tomatoes, celery, and green pepper. Chill. Before serving, add chopped tomato, celery, and green pepper.

Macaroni Cheese Salad

Jane Quinn
Bozeman, Montana

Like many of you, I started cooking before the pasta era. I made many huge batches of this salad. In fact, I have on occasion mixed it in a waste paper basket lined with a garbage bag. I also fixed a batch of this salad whenever we journeyed on gold-panning adventures with summer visitors. I fondly remember the hot dogs, brats, and Three-Bean salads that were part of the picnic menu. Brownies provided a tasty finale.

1	cup elbow macaroni, cooked, drained, and cooled
1 1/2	cups ham (tuna is a good substitute)
1	cup sharp cheddar cheese, cubed
1/2	cup celery slices, bias cut
1/3	cup green pepper, chopped
1/4	cup green onion, sliced
2	tablespoons pimento, chopped
1/4	cup pickle relish, drained
1/2	cup mayonnaise or salad dressing
1	tablespoon prepared mustard
1/4	teaspoon salt

Combine all ingredients except mayonnaise and mustard. Blend mayonnaise, mustard, and salt. Add to salad and toss lightly. Chill.

6 servings

Pasta Spinach Salad

Sharon Andriolo
Bozeman, Montana

Sharon is a skilled quilter and devoted wife, mother, and grandmother. Without any fanfare, Sharon takes care of ordering the notions and books at Quilting in the Country.

6	ounces rigatoni pasta
2	medium tomatoes, seeded and chopped
1/4	cup green onion, sliced
2	tablespoons black olives, sliced
1/2	cup feta cheese, crumbled
1/3	cup low-calorie Italian dressing
6	cups spinach, torn

Cook pasta. Drain. Gently toss with all ingredients except spinach. Chill.

To serve, arrange spinach on plates and spoon pasta mixture on top.

Serves 8

Lois' No-Name Salad

Lois Sicz
Bozeman, Montana

This is a great crisp and crunchy salad invented by Lois. It reminds me of a bright and cheery scrap quilt.

1	14-ounce package *Antoine's Fusilli Tricolor* pasta
1	16-ounce bottle *Kraft Fat Free Italian Dressing*
1	11-ounce can *Green Giant Mexicorn*
1	2 1/4-ounce can ripe olives, sliced
1/2	cup green bell pepper, chopped
1/2	cup red bell pepper, chopped
1/4	cup onion, chopped

Cook pasta according to package directions. Cool with cold water; drain well.

Add remaining ingredients, toss, and chill. Enjoy.

Noreen's Pasta Salad

Brenda R. Hauer - "All In Stitches"
Polson, Montana

1	pound penne pasta
1/2	pound feta cheese, crumbled
2	fresh tomatoes, diced
1/2	cup olive oil
2	tablespoons red wine vinegar
1	teaspoon oregano
	garlic, to taste
	fresh basil, to taste

Prepare pasta as directed on the package. Cool. Add remaining ingredients to pasta. Serve chilled.

Pasta Salad

Maren Kast
Willow Creek, Montana

Maren is a talented fiber artist and gallery owner in the tiny, charming town of
Willow Creek, Montana.

Salad:

1 pound pasta

1/4 cup olive oil

1 medium chili pepper, charred, peeled, and chopped

1 sweet pepper - red, green, or both, chopped

fresh broccoli florets, blanched

6 green onions, thinly sliced

3 cloves garlic, minced

fresh mushrooms, to taste

1 cup cheese, parmesan or peccorino-romano cheese, freshly grated

basil, to taste

Vinaigrette:

1/4 cup balsamic vinegar

1 tablespoon Dijon mustard

1 teaspoon sugar

1 clove garlic, minced

freshly ground pepper

basil, to taste

thyme, to taste

1/2 cup olive oil

Whisk together all vinaigrette ingredients, except olive oil. Slowly add olive oil.

Cook pasta al dente, drain, and toss with olive oil; cool. Mix pasta with vegetables and 3/4 cup cheese. Pour vinaigrette over pasta mixture and toss well. Garnish with remaining cheese and fresh basil.

Macaroni Salad

Maria Wolslagel
Bozeman, Montana

Maria is new to the Quilting in the Country staff and we really appreciate her as well as her organizational skills. Maria found this recipe in a cookbook her Aunt Hazel gave her when she got married. This is a hearty salad; good to serve with cold cuts or sandwiches and one that Maria's family always enjoys.

4	ounces macaroni
1/2	green pepper, finely chopped
1	large or 2 small tomatoes, finely chopped
1/2	cup celery, chopped
3/4	cup mayonnaise, diluted with vinegar and sugar to taste
	sprinkle of black pepper

Boil macaroni in salted water, drain, and chill. Toss remaining ingredients together, add macaroni, and serve.

Broccoli Tortellini

Kimberli Hart McCullough
Big Timber, Montana

This salad is always requested at Kimberli's parties with friends.
She recommends the fresh tortellini at Costco for this recipe.

1   7-ounce package fresh tortellini pasta

1   cup broccoli florets

1/2   cup fresh parsley, finely chopped

1   tablespoon pimento

1   6-ounce jar marinated artichoke hearts, undrained

2   green onions, sliced

2 1/2 teaspoons fresh basil

1/2   teaspoon garlic powder

1/2   cup prepared Italian dressing

5-6   cherry tomatoes, halved

      ripe olives, sliced

      parmesan cheese, grated

Cook pasta according to package directions. Drain and rinse with cold water. In a large bowl, combine all ingredients except cherry tomatoes, olives, and cheese. Cover and refrigerate 4-6 hours to blend the flavors. Before serving, add tomatoes; mix lightly. Garnish with olives and sprinkle with cheese.

Fettuccine Heaven Salad

Coco Beland
Bozeman, Montana

This recipe is fantastic at the height of tomato season!

Salad:

1 pound fettuccine, fresh if available

1 medium red onion, diced

1 3 1/2-ounce jar capers, drained

1 cup Greek olives, pitted and sliced

1 bunch basil sliced (leaves only)

1 bunch fresh spinach, coarsely chopped (leaves only)

3 pounds ripe tomatoes, diced

Dressing:

1/2 cup extra virgin olive oil

1 medium garlic clove, minced

2 tablespoons balsamic vinegar

1 teaspoon salt

  fresh ground pepper to taste

Shake dressing ingredients together.

Cook fettuccine al dente; drain and toss with dressing. Add onion, capers, olives, and basil. Just before serving, toss with spinach and transfer to a serving bowl lined with extra spinach leaves. Top with tomatoes and serve at room temperature.

Wilted Spinach and Pasta

Shannon Heffern
Scottsdale, Arizona

Shannon shares my dream of writing cookbooks. A registered dietician by trade, Shannon is an avid gardener who loves cooking. She'd like to combine these interests in a cookbook, but like many of us, finds herself in a "Catch-22" between making a living and pursuing her interests. Good luck, Shannon! We'll all be waiting for your cookbook!

Salad:

1	6-ounce package rotelle pasta
8	cups (10-ounces) spinach, torn
1/2	cup green onion, sliced
1/2	cup carrot, shredded
1/2	teaspoon black pepper

Dressing:

4-5	slices bacon, cut into 1-inch pieces
2	tablespoons white wine vinegar
1-2	tablespoons lemon juice
1	teaspoon sugar
	grated parmesan cheese

Cook pasta until al dente; rinse and drain. Combine pasta, spinach, green onion, and carrot. Sprinkle with pepper.

For dressing, cook bacon in a large skillet until crisp. Do not drain off drippings. Stir in vinegar, lemon juice, and sugar.

Pour the dressing over the spinach mixture. Toss lightly to coat. Sprinkle with cheese.

6-8 side dish servings

Cavatappi Oriental

Jill Binette
Great Falls, Montana

My friend, Jill Binette, originally invented this salad when serving lunch to the Chinese Ambassador who visited Pasta Montana in Great Falls last spring.

1	pound cooked cavatappi pasta (tubular corkscrew shape)
1	tablespoon sesame oil
1	bottle *Mrs. Chan's Oriental Dressing*, or any other oriental dressing
2	celery stalks, diced
1/2	pound green seedless grapes
2	garlic cloves, minced
1	bunch green onions, thinly chopped
1	chicken breast, cooked and shredded, or a can of white meat chicken
2	cans mandarin oranges, drained (juice reserved)
1/2	cup almond slivers, toasted (optional)

Cook pasta according to package directions. Toss with sesame oil. In a large bowl, mix dressing, celery, grapes, garlic, and green onions. Add chicken, toss again, add pasta, and toss once more. Gently fold in mandarin oranges; be careful, or they will disintegrate. Check the moisture level of your salad; and add the reserved mandarin orange juice if it seems too dry. Garnish with toasted almonds.

To learn to know one's self, to pursue the avenues of self-development is what I call creative aging-"
Stough

Garden Vegetable Rotini

Jill Binette
Great Falls, Montana

Jill made this salad for the 1999 Quilt Show volunteers just in case there were any vegetarians in the crowd. It could just as easily be made adding chicken or tuna for a light lunch dish.

1/2 cup olive oil, laced with 3 minced garlic cloves

1 pound tricolor rotini pasta

1 bottle Italian salad dressing

3 cups any combination of the following chopped vegetables: carrots, celery, green, red or yellow peppers, zucchini, yellow squash, green onions

Cook pasta according to package directions and toss with olive oil. Mix dressing, vegetables, and pasta, and serve.

Chicken Pasta

Jane Quinn
Bozeman, Montana

Salad:

1 1/4	pounds rainbow rotini, uncooked
1	pound cooked chicken breast
1/2	yellow onion, chopped
2	cups celery, chopped
1	red pepper, julienne cut
1	green pepper, julienne cut

Dressing:

4	cups mayonnaise
1/2	cup sour cream
2 1/2	teaspoons sugar
2 1/2	teaspoons garlic salt
2	teaspoons black pepper

Cook rotini, drain, and cool. Tear chicken into bite-size pieces. Prepare vegetables. Mix together dressing and combine with other ingredients. Chill and serve.

Mend a quarrel.
Seek out a forgotten friend.
Write a love letter.
Share some treasure.
Give a soft answer.
Encourage youth, keep a promise.
Find the time.
Forgive an enemy.
Listen.
Apologize if you were wrong.
Think first of someone else.
Be kind and gentle.
Laugh a little, laugh a little more.
Express your gratitude.
Gladden the heart of a child.
Take pleasure in the beauty and wonder of the earth.
Speak your love.
Speak it again.
Speak it still once more.

Greek Feta Salad

Jane Quinn
Bozeman, Montana

Salad:

1   pound medium-size pasta shells

1   cup celery, chopped

3/4   cup black olives, sliced

1/2   pound Greek feta cheese, crumbled

1/2   cup parmesan cheese, shredded

2   ripe tomatoes

Dressing:

1   cup heavy mayonnaise

3/4   cup Italian salad dressing

1   tablespoon dried oregano leaves

1   teaspoon black pepper

Cook pasta in plenty of water, al dente. Drain, and rinse well with cold water.

Whisk dressing ingredients together in a small bowl. Toss dressing with all ingredients (except tomatoes). Finally, chop tomatoes coarsely, and gently fold them into the salad.

Serves 8

Most of all the other beautiful things in life come by twos and threes, by dozens and hundreds. Plenty of roses, stars, sunsets, rainbows, brothers and sisters, aunts and cousins, but only one mother in the whole world.
Kate Douglas Wiggin

Tom's Pasta Salad

Barb Dena
Parachute, Colorado

This recipe comes from the man whom Barb says gave her the greatest quilting present ever - an undisclosed sum of money deposited at Quilting in the Country to use for quilting supplies and fabric. Barb was never to know the amount of the fund and I would let Tom know when the funds dwindled, so that he could add more to it. The gift went on for two years before Barb moved away. To this day, Barb does not how much was in the fund. I think that the Quilting in the Country staff had as much fun with this gift as Barb did! As for Tom, not only does he indulge Barb's quilting habit, but he can cook, too! I have to agree with Barb when she says that angels come in strange forms!

1	small package curly, colored macaroni
	small amount fresh broccoli, chopped
	small amount fresh cauliflower, finely chopped
1	green or red pepper, chopped
1	tablespoon vinegar
	pepper (to taste)
1	small package real parmesan cheese, grated
1	bottle parmesan pepper salad dressing

Cook macaroni until tender. Drain. Place in a large bowl. Chop vegetables and toss with vinegar to coat. Add vegetables to macaroni and pepper to taste. Last, mix in grated parmesan cheese and salad dressing.

Serves 4

Steak and Salad Penne

Jill Binette
Great Falls, Montana

Jill created this salad specifically for the 1999 Quilting in the Country Show volunteers.

1/2 cup olive oil, laced with 3 minced garlic cloves

1 pound penne pasta

1/2 pound cooked skirt steak, shredded (or any other steak that shreds well)

1/2 white onion, diced

1 bottle sun-dried tomato salad dressing

1 bag Italian salad greens

basil (optional)

Cook pasta according to package directions and toss with olive oil. In a large bowl, mix steak, onion, and dressing. Add salad greens and pasta. Toss. Garnish lightly with basil. Add additional dressing if needed.

RAMEN
SALADS

Dear Neighbors,
"To me Montana is a symphony - a symphony of color painted by a thousand different plants and shrubs which set the hills ablaze each with it's own inner fire." Mike Mansfield, November 8, 1989.

Autumn is my favorite time of the year. I love the weave of the colors. I slow my pace after the quilt show. The sights and sounds of autumn are so wonderful. The leaves turn color and sunlit days become shorter. I let summer slip away, but it's a little sad, seeing the landscape turn brown, so I make every effort to eat the last vegetables from the garden and smell the good smells of growing plants and the hayfield. The green drains away. The frost hits. As a child I remember hearing the dry cornstalks shaking in the wind as if they were shivering; pumpkins would provide the only remaining color.

I grew up on a farm in Iowa and every Fall brings back memories of harvest for me. Images of corn, tractors and late summer evenings are indelibly printed on my mind this time of year.

But just as harvest means a change of season, it also signals the spirit of sharing. Life on the farm would have been incomplete without our "neighbors" down the road. Many of life's lessons came from our neighbors. In a small community everyone knew everyone else's business. They knew your grandparents, aunts and uncles. It seemed to me they knew who your boyfriend was and maybe even the grade you got on your last algebra test! These disadvantages could be overlooked because those neighbors really cared.

We came to depend on our neighbors, and they on us, every time of the year, but especially during the harvest. Each person made a difference. When I was 5 years old our barn burned down while we were away on family vacation. I recall very clearly our neighbor calling to tell us. As we rushed home we felt confident everything was under control. With winter approaching, the neighbors helped build a new barn. In my teenage years my father was diagnosed with multiple sclerosis. Again the neighbors rallied and helped my family for many years. They cared.

I meet the Fall with my usual thoughts of harvest, but also pause to think back over the past summer months. I am thankful beyond words to all of you who helped make "Quilting in the Country" one of the ten best quilt shops in America; accepting the award in St. Louis at Quilt Market was perhaps my proudest professional achievement. Summer also brought with it the death of my father-in-law - that was the first chance for my husband's family to gain that feeling of support that comes from a valued circle of friendship. Those neighbors came forth with food and meaningful sentiments at another passage of life. When our daughter became dangerously ill after the birth of our grandson, her neighbors in Denver came to the rescue.

As we enter another season and I remember my ties to a way of life based on neighborliness, I appreciate even more, you, my neighbors at "Quilting in the Country." I am ever mindful that while technology gives us many wonderful things and certainly makes our lives simpler and faster, we cannot afford to lose the human touch that made life on the farm unique.

Enjoy the texture, the color and the harmony of autumn. I hope to see you soon.

Your neighbor,

Jane

Summertime Coleslaw

Kelly Kelsey
Bozeman, Montana

Kelly and her husband, Kim, own Nine Quarter Circle Ranch in the Gallatin Canyon. Kelly hosts a quilter's retreat every September at the ranch. The meals served there are quite tasty! Kelly likes this salad as a summertime main dish with a loaf of crusty French bread.

Salad:

3 cups green cabbage, shredded

2 cups red cabbage, shredded

2 large red or yellow peppers, thinly sliced or diced

2 carrots, matchstick size

8 green onions, matchstick size or diagonally-cut

1/2 cup fresh cilantro, chopped

salt and pepper

Dressing:

6 tablespoons rice vinegar

6 tablespoons vegetable oil

5 tablespoons creamy peanut butter

5 tablespoons soy sauce

3 tablespoons brown sugar, packed

2 tablespoons fresh ginger, minced

1 1/2 tablespoons garlic, minced

Whisk all dressing ingredients together. (Dressing can be made one day ahead.) Cover and chill. Let dressing stand at room temperature 30 minutes before adding to vegetables. Toss salad vegetables with dressing to coat. Season with salt and pepper.

Noodle Salad

Jo Ireland
Bozeman, Montana

Jo is a great quilting woman and a great cook!

2 packages (3-ounces each) instant Asian noodle soup mix, such as *Top Ramen*

2 tablespoons white vinegar

2 tablespoons lime juice

2 tablespoons sugar

2 teaspoons Asian sesame oil

1/8 teaspoon hot chili flakes

1/4 teaspoon salt

1/2 cup cilantro leaves or parsley, chopped

3/4 cup carrot, grated

3/4 cup zucchini, grated

1/2 cup dry roasted peanuts (use 3/4 cup if preferred)

Break up dry noodles while still in the package, discard seasoning packets. Bring 2 quarts of water to a boil over high heat. Add noodles and cook about 3 minutes. Rinse noodles in cold water and drain.

In a salad bowl, add vinegar, lime juice, sugar, oil, chili flakes, and salt. Stir until sugar dissolves. Add noodles, cilantro, carrot, zucchini, and peanuts. Mix ingredients. Serve or chill up to 4 hours.

6 servings

Chestnut and cider, sorrel and roan ~ the very colors that add beauty to field and farm make wonderful shades for quilts too.

Cabbage Ramen Noodles Salad

Pat Walter
Pine Island, Minnesota

I received three variations of this yummy salad! (The variations follow this recipe.)

Salad:

2　packages beef-flavored ramen noodles

1　pound cabbage, shredded

1　green onion, chopped

1　cup sunflower seeds

1　cup toasted slivered almonds

Dressing:

3/4　cup canola oil

1/3　cup vinegar

1/2　cup sugar

　　flavor packets from ramen noodles

Break noodles up into small pieces. Combine salad ingredients. Mix dressing well and pour over cabbage mixture just before serving.

Broccoli Cole Slaw

Sharon Lesperance
Trenton, Mississippi

To make this variation, use 1 pound package broccoli coleslaw instead of the cabbage. Substitute 2 oriental-flavor ramen noodles for the beef noodles, and use 1/4 cup slivered almonds and 3 chopped green onions. Pour dressing over the salad and refrigerate overnight. Toss before serving.

Patti's Bernina Cabbage Salad

"Patti's Bernina"
Sunburst, Montana

For this variation, use 1/2 head chopped cabbage, 1/2 cup slivered almonds, 2 tablespoons sunflower seeds, 4 green onions, and 1 package chicken flavored ramen noodles. The dressing calls for 1/3 cup oil, 3 tablespoons vinegar, 2 tablespoons sugar, 1/2 teaspoon pepper, and the ramen flavoring packet. Mix dressing ingredients well, pour over salad mixture, and serve.

Texas Pan Handle Cabbage Salad

Sue Spargo
Salt Lake City, Utah

Sue is one of our favorite authors of folk inspired block of the month, Country Days.

1	head Chinese cabbage
8-10	green onions
1	medium bell pepper, chopped
2	packages chicken flavored ramen noodles
3/4	cup slivered almonds
1/2	cup sesame seeds

Dressing:

1	cup vegetable oil
2/3	cup sugar
1/3	cup rice wine vinegar
1/2	teaspoon pepper

Brown crushed noodles, almonds and seeds in 2 tablespoons margarine, until lightly browned

Cool and sprinkle with seasoning packet from noodles. Place in container, separate from greens

Mix dressing in container and seal. Chop cabbage, green onion and bell pepper. Mix and refrigerate. Toss all ingredients together just before serving.

This makes quite a large salad. For a smaller serving, make half of each mixture and/or save in separate containers, as the noodles become soggy when mixed ahead of time.

Easy Coleslaw
"Patti's Bernina"
Sunburst, Montana

Salad:
- 1   head cabbage, chopped
- 1   medium-size onion, chopped
- 1/2   green pepper, chopped
- 3/4   cup sugar

Dressing:
- 1/2   cup vinegar
- 1/2   cup oil
- 1   teaspoon salt
- 1   teaspoon celery seed

Pour sugar over salad ingredients, do not stir. Mix dressing ingredients in a small saucepan and bring to a boil. Pour dressing over the cabbage mixture and refrigerate until ready to eat. Do not stir salad at any time during preparation.

Bok Choy Salad
Rose McCaig
Pointe Claire, Quebec, Canada

- 1   head bok choy, chopped
- 1   bunch green onions, chopped
- 12   mushrooms, sliced
-     seasoned rice vinegar
-     oil
-     sugar
-     toasted almonds
-     canned ramen noodles

Mix bok choy, green onions, and mushrooms. Make dressing with vinegar, oil, and sugar. (Quantities depend on size of head of bok choy). Mix dressing thoroughly with bok choy mixture. Add toasted almonds and add the ramen noodles just before serving.

Jennifer's Chinese Noodle Salad

Barb Dena
Parachute, Colorado

Barb has a joke in her family that her son will not eat anything ending in "eese" unless it is Wendy's. Therefore, this is her daughter's salad.

Salad:

1　large head cabbage, chopped

5-7　green onions with tops, finely chopped

1　small package slivered almonds (2-ounces)

　　sesame seeds, to taste

2　packages ramen noodles (discard flavor packets), broken up

1/2　cup margarine (maximum) begin with 2 tablespoons

Dressing:

1/2　cup salad oil

2　teaspoons soy sauce

1/2　cup sugar

1/2　cup wine vinegar

Chop cabbage and onion, combine and chill. Brown noodles, sesame seeds, and almonds in the margarine until lightly browned. Mix dressing ingredients well. About 20 - 30 minutes before serving, combine cabbage and noodle mix, top with dressing.

Serves 4-6

There is a fountain of youth: it is your mind, your talents, the creativity you bring to your life. Loren

VEGGIE SALADS

My friends, I have a special friend. We met over a bolt of yucky green cotton. She was carrying the most wonderful Antique Log Cabin quilt. We were kindred spirits from the beginning. Recently I came upon a card this friend had sent me some time ago. The card contained this greeting: "Every once in a while we find a friend who cares as much as we care, someone to share what we share, someone who likes the things we do... Every once in a while we find someone like you." And she added, "my special kindred spirit friend." And in the enclosed letter she wrote, "I kept looking for a few quiet moments so I could compose this wonderful letter to tell you how much our friendship means to me and how I value your creative input in my life. Well, no quiet moments and no wonderful letter, but I do want you to know how I feel about being best friends. I wish we had more time for quality visits - doing things together, like we used to at the beginning - the things that deepen friendship. But when we're old and gray maybe we can rock and quilt together! Right now I guess we'll take whatever we can get!" The handwritten words said many special things but the most important was acknowledging that she was thinking only of me and our friendship. You have friends like that, I'm sure.

I have another very special friend. We were both born and raised on farms in Iowa. We met when we were very young. Our mothers had been high school classmates and my friend's grandmother lived in our neighborhood. We share so many things in common. We were active 4-H members. I was elected county president. She was the secretary. She was the valedictorian of our class. I was in the top ten! There was never any jealousy or bitterness in our relationship. We shared each others joy all the way. We double dated, loved sewing and playing in the band. We kept contact with each other even though we attended different colleges. Our friendship has been a long term solid one. The homes we have lived in since marriage are similar in many ways - older, self-remodeled ones. On a family vacation we had acquired an antique commode from my grandparents. Bill was mildly protesting carrying it back to Montana. He really could see no good use for it and I think he was privately revolted when I told him I thought it would make a good coffee table. With the commode in the trunk of our car, we stopped to visit my friend. It was amazing to find a nearly identical commode already in use as a coffee table in her living room!. Recently, my friend and her husband made a trip hundreds of miles out of their way just to get together for morning coffee. And over the years, our husbands have grown to be friends also.

"The Country of the Pointed Firs," written by Sarah Orne Jewett, contains this conversation between two friends: "There, it does seem so pleasant to talk with an old acquaintance that knows what you know. Conversations got to have some root in the past or else you've got to explain every remark you make and it wears a person out," says the one. Her friend relies; "Yes'm old friends is always best, lest you catch a new one to make an old one out of."

Sociologists provide these facts and figures: The average adult has 1-2 best friends, 4-6 close friends, and anywhere from 10 to 20 casual friends. It takes on the average 3 years to form lasting friendships. People have the least friends during their middle ages and the most friends during young adulthood and old age.

It is difficult to find time to maintain friendships in our overly busy lives but it is one of the best things we can do for ourselves. It is proven that having friends for life helps us to stay healthier, happier and live longer lives. Studies have proven that the most important factor in wellness is connection with friends and organizations. When we have close relationships we even have fewer colds!

Some months ago my friend and I decided to give each other the gift of getting together 2 days a month. We put each other's name on a calendar and try to let nothing interfere with those days. Oh, we say it's because we're too overwhelmed with unfinished quilting projects, but the truth is being together reinforces and strengthens the positive things in life. Sharing moments (happy or unhappy ones) builds our sense of security and communicates that we are persons of worth and value. Quilting provides a reason for friends to get together. How fortunate we are to have this connection.

I hope you have a friend who accepts you as you are and with which there is no pretense. Old friends have been through a lot together and will do anything for one another. As I grow older the simple pleasures of life become even more important. Keeping up with old friends should be top priority. Seasons end but why not create new beginnings? Ask a friend to come quilting or take a quilting class with you? It's good for you both and it's fun! Jane

Tomato, Mozzarella, and Basil Salad

Anne Quinn Egan and Julie Bush Maletic
Denver, Colorado

This salad is a favorite of my daughter, Anne, and our good friend, Julie Bush Maletic.

Salad:

1 large tomato, cut into
1/4-inch slices

1/4 pound fresh mozzarella
cheese, cut into
1/4-inch slices

6-8 large fresh basil leaves,
thinly sliced

Dressing:

1 tablespoon olive oil

3 tablespoons balsamic
vinegar

1 teaspoon garlic, minced

1/4 teaspoon English
dry mustard

1/8 teaspoon sugar

In a small bowl, whisk dressing
ingredients together, adding salt
and pepper to taste. On a platter,
arrange tomato slices alternately
with mozzarella and top with
basil. Drizzle salad with
dressing. Serve.

Serves 2

Italian Vegetable Salad

Shirley Drake Naismith
Grand Forks, North Dakota

Grandmother Shirley provides inspiration for her quilting relatives - including granddaughter Clara Bergene and daughter Jean Gullicks.

Salad:

1 large head cauliflower, chunked

2 bunches broccoli, chunked

2 green peppers, chunked

1 1/2 cups celery, chopped

1 cup onion, chopped

6 carrots, chunked

1 can pitted black olives, drained (reserve juice)

1 pound box cherry tomatoes

Dressing:

1 3/4 cups cider vinegar

juice from olives

1 1/2 cups water

1 1/2 cups salad oil

3/4 cup white sugar

1 teaspoon black pepper

3 teaspoons salt

2 tablespoons paprika

1/2 teaspoon garlic powder

Blend dressing ingredients until well mixed. Marinate salad ingredients for 24 hours in dressing, tossing occasionally. Serve on a bed of mixed lettuce greens.

Clara's Garden Salad

Clara Naismith Bergene, Age 8
Fridley, Minnesota

Clara stopped by with her aunt, Sara Gullicks, last March. They were on a ski trip. Clara entered a quilt in the Minnesota quilt show and at age 8, she was not the youngest quiltmaker - her 5 year old sister Christine was! Clara says that these vegetables are best picked fresh from Grandma and Grandpa's garden. Yummy!

cherry tomatoes or
sliced tomatoes

cucumbers, cut in strips

red and yellow
peppers, sliced

lettuce leaves

chunky bleu cheese
salad dressing

Mix tomatoes, cucumbers, and peppers and serve on a bed of lettuce leaves. Dip vegetables in bleu cheese dressing.

Sweet Potato Salad

Cydell Chambers
Bozeman, Montana

Make this salad a day ahead to improve the flavor.

2   1-pound cans
     sweet potatoes

4   hard-boiled eggs,
     chopped

4   green onions,
     finely chopped

1 1/2 cups celery,
     finely chopped

1/2 teaspoon salt

1/2 cup Durkee's
     salad dressing

1/2 cup mayonnaise

Thoroughly mash the potatoes and eggs. Combine with other ingredients. Cover tightly and refrigerate.

Serves 10-12

Very Pretty Salad

Coco Beland
Bozeman, Montana

*Coco not only makes clever and unique clothing and quilted projects -
she is a great cook.*

Salad:

1   yellow pepper,
     seeded and sliced

1   red pepper,
     seeded and sliced

1/2 pound fresh snow peas,
     blanched for one minute

1/2 pound fresh mushrooms,
     cleaned and sliced

2   tablespoons toasted
     sesame seeds

Dressing:

2   tablespoons sesame
     seed oil

4   tablespoons seasoned
     rice wine vinegar

1/2 teaspoon salt

1   teaspoon fresh
     ground pepper

1/4 cup vegetable oil

Shake dressing ingredients together in a covered jar. Toss all vegetables with just enough dressing to coat, and sprinkle with toasted sesame seeds.

Chevre Stuffed Portobello Mushrooms on a Bed of Greens

Julie Bush Maletic
Denver, Colorado

Julie grew up in Bozeman. Both Julie and her mother, Wendy, are creative and inspiring friends. We tease Julie that she's the Martha Stewart of the West! For this elegant salad, there will be some vinaigrette remaining, which can be used for other purposes.

Salad:

4	Portobello mushrooms, cleaned with stems removed
8	ounces Chevre (soft, mild goat cheese)
10	cups mixed baby salad greens
2	roasted red peppers, cut into strips

Balsamic Vinaigrette:

2	tablespoons balsamic vinegar
1	tablespoon red wine vinegar
1	tablespoon Dijon mustard
1	garlic clove, crushed
1/2	teaspoon salt
1/4	teaspoon freshly ground black pepper
3/4	cup extra virgin olive oil

To make the vinaigrette, whisk all ingredients, except oil, in a bowl until mixed. Gradually whisk in the oil until combined.

Preheat oven to 400 degrees. Brush all sides of mushrooms with vinaigrette. Slice Chevre into 16 equal discs and place four discs into each mushroom cap, gill side up. Bake on top rack of oven for 8-10 minutes, or until sizzling and cheese begins to melt.

Toss mixed greens with vinaigrette. Divide greens between four plates. Top each with quartered stuffed Portobello caps. Garnish with roasted red pepper strips.

Cheese Tomato Salad

Eleanor Christian
Bozeman, Montana

Eleanor quilted in a group with a dear neighbor friend of mine, Jane Edie.
I imagine she brought this salad when the group shared potluck together.

1	tablespoon plus 1 teaspoon Knox Gelatin
1/4	cup cold water
1	can tomato soup, heated
1	cup cottage cheese
1/2	cup mayonnaise
1/2	cup whipping cream
1/3	cup celery, chopped
1/3	cup onion, chopped
1/3	cup green pepper, chopped

Dissolve gelatin well in cold water. Add tomato soup, cottage cheese, and mayonnaise to gelatin mixture. Whip cream, adding some salt. Fold in celery, onion, and green pepper. Combine gelatin mixture with cream mixture. Pour into mold. Refrigerate well.

10 servings

Mock Crab Salad

Joan Hodgeboom, "Quilt Gallery"
Kalispell, Montana

Joan is a friend and owner of a premier shop in Kalispell. The shop is
housed in a building that was once home to an elegant bar. In Joan's unusual
salad, pimento gives the parsnips a pink tinge.

2	large parsnips
1	cup celery, diced
1	medium onion, chopped
2	tablespoons pimento, chopped
2	tablespoons pickle, chopped
1/2	cup mayonnaise (or Thousand Island salad dressing)

Wash and peel parsnips, grind coarsely. Add celery, onion, pickle, and pimento; mix, stir in mayonnaise and seasonings, to taste.

Pam's Cucumbers

Pam Bauer
Exira, Iowa

Pam is my sister-in-law. When we visit Exira, she spoils us with the greatest food. When Pam and my brother, Dean, were first married, Dean introduced Pam's cucumbers to us with the statement, "You're going to love these!"

onions	Peel and slice onions and cucumbers, using fewer onions than cucumbers. Cover with water and sprinkle with several tablespoons salt. Soak several hours. Drain, and rinse.
cucumbers	
salt and pepper	
white vinegar	
sugar	

Make a brine of equal parts water, white vinegar, and sugar - enough to cover the cucumbers and onions. (Pam starts with 3/4 cup of each.) Add salt and pepper to taste. These cucumbers only get better when stored in the refrigerator. Never fear - they won't last long!

"What is the secret of your life?"
asked Mrs. Browning of Charles Kingsley.
"Tell me, that I may make mine beautiful too."
He replied, "I had a friend." William C. Gannet

Moldavian Potato Salad

Joan Hodgeboom, "Quilt Gallery"
Kalispell, Montana

Joan's sister-in-law makes this salad for her family and Joan's. Joan doesn't enjoy cooking, but says her sister-in-law is a great cook.

6	medium red skinned potatoes
1/3	cup olive oil
2	cloves garlic, chopped fine
1	cup (about 8-ounces) feta cheese, crumbled
1/4	cup scallions, chopped
3	tablespoons wine vinegar
2	tablespoons dill, preferably fresh
	salt (to taste)
	pepper (to taste)
	black olives for garnish

Boil potatoes until tender. When cool enough to handle, cut them into 3/4 inch pieces. Combine olive oil and garlic; toss potatoes in the mixture. Cool to room temperature. Add the rest of the ingredients and allow salad to sit for at least 1 hour before serving.

Vegetable Salad

Robin Stilwell, "Quilt-essentials"
Butte, Montana

Recently a friend shared a clipping from the summer kids' quilting classes at Quilt-essentials. Young children make dozens of quilts for charity. Thanks to Robin for passing on the tradition.

Salad:

1   15-ounce can shoe peg corn, drained

1   15-ounce can cut green beans, drained and cut smaller if desired

1   small package frozen peas

1   medium red bell pepper, chopped

1   cup celery, chopped

1   medium green pepper, chopped

1   bunch green onion, chopped

Dressing:

1/2   cup oil

3/4   cup vinegar

1   cup sugar

1   teaspoon salt

1   teaspoon pepper

1   tablespoon water

For dressing, bring all ingredients to a boil and cool. Mix vegetables with dressing and refrigerate overnight - 2 days is even better.

Broccoli-Mandarin Salad

Marian Neill
Whitehall, Montana

Salad:

4	cups fresh broccoli florets
1/2	cup raisins
6	slices bacon, cooked and crumbled
2	cups fresh mushrooms, sliced
1/2	cup slivered almonds, toasted
1	11-ounce can mandarin oranges, drained
1/2	red onion, thinly sliced

Dressing:

1	egg plus 1 egg yolk, lightly beaten
1/2	cup sugar
1 1/2	teaspoons cornstarch
1	teaspoon dry mustard
1/4	cup tarragon vinegar
1/4	cup water
3	tablespoons butter
1/2	cup mayonnaise

To make dressing, whisk eggs, sugar, cornstarch, and mustard in top of a double boiler over hot water. Combine vinegar and water. Slowly pour into egg mixture, stirring constantly. Cook, continue stirring, until mixture thickens. Remove from heat; stir in butter and mayonnaise. Chill. Toss dressing with salad ingredients and serve.

Bacon, Tomato, and Potato Salad

Jane Quinn
Bozeman, Montana

Salad:

2 1/2 pounds small red potatoes

2 cups celery, chopped

1/2 green pepper, julienne 1/4-inch thick

1/4 yellow onion, minced

1 cup bacon bits

1 1/2 tomatoes, chopped

Dressing:

1/2 cup mayonnaise

1/2 cup sour cream

1 tablespoon Dijon mustard

1 tablespoon white vinegar

1/2 tablespoon salt

1/2 teaspoon black pepper, coarsely ground

Steam potatoes, cool, and quarter. Toss together potatoes, celery, green pepper, onion, and bacon bits. In a separate bowl, make dressing. Gently mix dressing into potato mixture. Chill. Just before serving, mix in tomatoes.

When you quilt to please yourself; it tends to please others, too.

Pickled Beet and Walnut Salad

Jane Quinn
Bozeman, Montana

I like the unique flavor that beets give this salad!

1   bunch fresh watercress
     or 2 cups Romaine
     lettuce, shredded

1   16-ounce jar whole
     pickle beets, halved
     and quartered

1   11-ounce can
     mandarin orange
     segments, drained

1   small sweet onion,
     thinly sliced and
     separated into rings

1/4 cup toasted walnuts,
     coarsely chopped

3/4 cup Newman's Own
     Olive Oil and
     Vinegar Dressing

Arrange first 3 ingredients on a watercress-lined platter. Just before serving, sprinkle with walnuts, and drizzle with dressing. Serve immediately.

6 servings

Baked German Potato Salad

Jane Quinn
Bozeman, Montana

3/4 cup bacon, diced	Cook bacon in a large skillet.
1 cup celery, chopped	Drain all but 1/4 cup of bacon
1 cup onion, chopped	grease. Remove bacon to paper towel lined plate. Add celery and
3 tablespoons flour	onion; cook one minute. Blend in
1 1/3 cups water	flour. Stir in water and vinegar;
2/3 cup cider vinegar	cook, stirring constantly, until mixture is thick and bubbly. Stir
2/3 cup sugar	in sugar, salt, and pepper. Using a
3 teaspoons salt	greased 3-quart casserole dish,
1/2 teaspoon pepper	pour mixture over potatoes and
8 cups (8 medium) potatoes, cooked and cubed	bacon and mix lightly. Cover and bake at 350 degrees for 30 minutes. Remove from oven and stir in radishes and dill pickle.
1 cup radishes, sliced	Serve at once.
1/2 cup dill pickle, chopped (optional)	*10-12 servings*

Victory Garden

Jane Quinn
Bozeman, Montana

Maybe it is my Iowa roots, but I think nothing beats the taste of fresh tomatoes!

2 pounds (2 quarts) garden tomatoes	Make dressing by combining pickling spice, white wine vinegar,
2 cloves garlic	water and kosher salt. Bring to a
1 tablespoon pickling spice	boil. Cool and pour over tomatoes and garlic. Weight the tomatoes
1/2 cup white wine vinegar	with a plate so they are completely
1 quart water	covered with dressing. Refrigerate
3 tablespoons kosher salt	for 24 hours before serving.

Broccoli Salad

Jeanette Quinn
Donahue, Iowa

My mother-in-law, Jeanette, always prepares wonderful meals whenever we visit the farm.

2   bunches broccoli or pea pods
1   cup celery, chopped
1   can water chestnuts, drained and sliced
1   can ripe olives
1   small bottle Italian salad dressing
1   package dry Italian salad dressing
1   bunch green onions, chopped
2   tomatoes, coarsely chopped

Marinate first 4 ingredients in both bottled and dry salad dressings. In the morning, add the green onions and tomatoes.

Vegetable Sauerkraut Salad

Debbie Seward, "All In Stitches"
Polson, Montana

1   29-ounce can sauerkraut
1   cup green pepper, chopped
1/2   cup onion, chopped
1/2   cup celery, chopped
1   small jar pimento, chopped
1/2   cup salad oil
1/2   cup sugar
1/2   cup vinegar

Rinse and drain sauerkraut in a large bowl; mix with other vegetables. In a saucepan, heat vinegar, sugar, and salad oil until sugar is dissolved. Pour dressing over the vegetables and let stand in refrigerator for 24 hours. Keeps well.

Serves 10-12

Sweet Potato Salad

Dorothy Kern
Bozeman, Montana

When we moved to Montana 30 years ago, everyone raved about the sweet potato salad from Lydia's restaurant in Butte, and claimed they had the original recipe!

Salad:

4 1/2 cups sweet potatoes, cooked (Dorothy thinks Taylor's sweet potatoes are the best for this recipe)

3-4 hard boiled eggs

2 bunches green onions, chopped

2 celery stalks, finely chopped

Dressing:

1/2 cup Best Foods mayonnaise (use 3/4 cup if preferred)

1/4 cup Durkees (use 1/2 cup if preferred)

1 teaspoon sweet pickle juice

2 tablespoons sugar

2 tablespoons brown sugar

2 tablespoons vinegar (apple cider vinegar)

2 tablespoons cream or milk

1/4 teaspoon mustard

1/4 teaspoon salt

1/4 teaspoon pepper

Mash sweet potatoes and eggs together. Add chopped onions and celery; mix. Add dressing and stir.

Cauliflower Salad

Patti's Bernina
Sunburst, Montana

Vary the vinegar in this salad - it creates a new taste each time!

Salad:

4 cups raw cauliflower, thinly sliced

1 cup ripe olives, coarsely chopped

1 1/2 cups green pepper, chopped

1/2 cup pimento, chopped

1/2 cup onion, chopped

Dressing:

1/2 cup salad oil

1/2 teaspoon sugar

3 tablespoons lemon juice

1/4 teaspoon pepper

3 tablespoons vinegar

salt

Put all salad ingredients in a medium-size bowl. Beat dressing ingredients with a rotary beater until well blended. Pour dressing over ingredients in the salad bowl and refrigerate, covered, about 4 hours or until well chilled. Chilling overnight works great.

Serves 8-10

Sweet and Sour Cucumbers with Onions

Kathy Center
Bozeman, Montana

This is a must-have recipe if you grow cucumbers in your garden!

2	cups cucumbers, pared and thinly sliced
1/2	teaspoon salt
1	cup onions, thinly sliced
1/4	cup vinegar
1	tablespoon water
1	tablespoon sugar
1/2	teaspoon dill weed
1/4	teaspoon cracked black pepper
	dash ground red pepper

Place cucumber slices in a bowl. Sprinkle with salt and cover with cold water. Refrigerate 30 minutes; drain well. Add onions, combine vinegar, water, sugar, dill weed, cracked black pepper, and red pepper. Pour over cucumbers and onions; toss lightly. Chill 1 hour or longer, tossing occasionally, before serving.

Serves 4

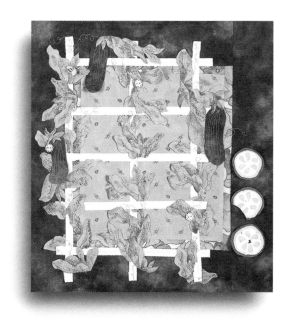

Wild Mushroom Salad

Malinda Ringo
Denver, Colorado

6	plum tomatoes
	salt and pepper, to taste
1/2	cup olive oil
1	teaspoon fresh rosemary, chopped
20	baby leeks or scallions
1	clove garlic, chopped
1	pound assorted fresh wild mushrooms (morels, chanterelles, shitake, etc.)
	sherry vinegar, to taste
	salt and pepper, to taste

Quarter the tomatoes. Season them with salt and pepper, a little of the olive oil, and half of the chopped rosemary. Roast in a 400 degree oven for 7 minutes.

Clean the scallion, coat with 2 teaspoons olive oil, salt, and pepper. Place on grill until charred and soft.

Slice and clean wild mushrooms and saute with olive oil and chopped garlic. When almost cooked, add sherry vinegar and salt and pepper to taste. Place the wild mushrooms as the base, with scallions on top, and roasted tomatoes around all. Sprinkle with remaining chopped rosemary and olive oil. Serve salad warm or at room temperature.

In the early autumn, eager for a change of pace,
I move my sewing machine outside.
The sunlight is softer, making it an ideal place to sew.

Easter Brunch Asparagus

Jane Quinn
Bozeman, Montana

Yes, this is a traditional part of our Easter brunch that includes Texas Eggs, ham, and an adult Easter egg hunt.

2 pounds asparagus
1 teaspoon garlic, minced
1/2 teaspoon salt
1/2 teaspoon white pepper
2 teaspoons Dijon mustard
1 1/2 teaspoons fresh lemon juice
3 tablespoons sesame oil
1 tablespoon toasted sesame seeds (for garnish)

Steam asparagus. Blend remaining ingredients. Marinate asparagus with dressing in a Ziplock bag overnight. Choose a serving platter to compliment the impressive, long stalks of asparagus.

Quick Salsa Salad

Juli Rognlie
Bozeman, Montana

Juli taught high school math before she quit to spend more time with her young daughters and help at Quilting in the Country.

1 15-ounce can corn, drained
1 15-ounce can black beans, rinsed
1 1/2 cups celery, chopped
1/2 cup green onion, chopped
1/4 cup fresh cilantro, minced
1 14-ounce jar salsa
1/4 cup red wine vinegar

Stir all ingredients together and chill.

Carrot Marinade Salad

Jane Quinn
Bozeman, Montana

This recipe came from my friend, Jane Edie. It is best made ahead and can be kept in the refrigerator for a long time. When the vegetables are gone, I use the remaining dressing on greens.

Salad:

2   pounds carrots, cooked until barely tender and cut into 1 1/2" bias slices

2   green peppers, seeded and sliced in rings

2   onions, sliced

Dressing:

1   cup sugar

1/2 cup cider vinegar

1/2 cup salad oil

1   can undiluted cream of tomato soup

1/2 teaspoon salt

1/2 teaspoon pepper

1/2 teaspoon dill, or dill seed

Blend ingredients for dressing in a blender or mixer. In a bowl, alternate layers of carrots, onion, green pepper, and blended dressing. Cover and refrigerate 12-24 hours.

Sour Cream Potato Salad

Corrine Hoffart
Bozeman, Montana

1/3 cup clear Italian salad dressing

7 medium (6 cups) potatoes, cooked in jackets, peeled, and sliced

3/4 cup celery, sliced

1/3 cup green onions, sliced

4 hard-cooked eggs

1 cup mayonnaise

1/2 cup dairy sour cream

1 1/2 teaspoons prepared horseradish, or mustard and horseradish

salt, to taste

celery seed, to taste

1/3 cup pared cucumber, diced (optional)

Pour dressing over warm potatoes; chill 2 hours. Add celery and onion. Chop egg whites and add to mixture. Sieve egg yolks; mix with mayonnaise, sour cream, and horseradish mustard. Fold into the salad. Add salt and celery seed to taste. Chill two hours. Add pared cucumber, if desired.

Makes 8 servings

Tomatoes Lutece

Lori Tonnsen
Billings, Montana

Long before her quilting days, a friend in Denver gave Lori this recipe. The recipe is 30 plus years old and still a summer favorite for garden tomatoes. Lori says the tomatoes always bring raves - even from friends who are not fond of tomatoes. She recommends the "fresh" tomatoes from Costco for this recipe. She says they taste like the real thing and work well to bring out the delicious flavor of the dressing, but be sure to peel them and use the dressing sparingly since the juices combine with the tomatoes.

firm, ripe tomatoes, peeled (dip them in hot water to peel them more easily)

cucumbers (optional)

onion slices (optional)

lettuce leaves (optional)

Dressing:

1/4	cup parsley, chopped
1	clove garlic, crushed
1	teaspoon salt
1	teaspoon sugar
1/4	teaspoon pepper
1/4	cup salad oil
2	tablespoons wine vinegar (or cider vinegar)
2	teaspoons prepared mustard

Shake dressing ingredients together in a jar. Slice each skinned tomato crosswise into 1/2-inch slices, re-form into a tomato shape again, and place in a shallow serving dish. Sparingly pour dressing over and into tomatoes.

Cover serving dish and chill at least an hour or more. Let stand at room temperature at least 20 minutes before serving. If you have any leftover tomatoes, chill and serve the next day. (Sometimes Lori adds fresh cucumbers and onion slices and serves tomatoes on a bed of lettuce leaves.)

New Potato Salad

Kay Davidson
Bozeman, Montana

This recipe is from Kay's son, Bryan Beneke, a student at the Culinary Institute of America. An interior designer, Kay adds a special touch to each of her quilts.

Salad:

1   pound red skin potatoes

2   red peppers

    vegetable oil

Dressing:

8   leaves Thai
    basil, chiffonade

1   tablespoon Grey Poupon
    Dijon mustard

3   tablespoons balsamic
    vinegar

6   tablespoons extra virgin
    olive oil

1   clove garlic,
    freshly minced

1   shallot, minced

1/2 teaspoon cayenne pepper

    salt and pepper to taste

Boil potatoes just until fork tender. Quarter and cool at room temperature. Rub peppers with vegetable oil and roast under broiler. After roasted, place in a bowl covered with plastic wrap for 5 minutes. Peel by hand or with a paring knife. De-seed and chop small - do not run under water.

Mix all dressing ingredients together. Coat all potatoes and roasted potatoes with dressing.

Broccoli and Bacon Salad

Barb Cribb
Bozeman, Montana

Barb calls this the perfect potluck salad and says not to be surprised when your friends call the next day and ask you for the recipe!

Salad:

2   large fresh raw broccoli flowerets, finely chopped

1/2 pound cooked bacon, cut in small pieces

3/4 cup golden raisins

1/4 cup red onion, finely chopped

1/2 cup peanuts

Dressing:

mayonnaise

vinegar

sugar

Mix all salad ingredients together in a large bowl. For dressing, mix mayonnaise, vinegar, and sugar together to taste. Pour dressing over salad, toss, and refrigerate.

Peggy's German Potato Salad

Peggy Lipsey
Bozeman, Montana

6	bacon slices
3/4	cup onion
2	tablespoons flour
2	tablespoons sugar
2	teaspoons salt
1/2	teaspoon celery seed
	dash pepper
3/4	cup water
1/3	cup vinegar
7	medium potatoes, cooked with skins on

In a large skillet, fry bacon until crisp. Remove to a paper towel and drain. Cook onion in bacon drippings until tender. Stir in flour, sugar, salt, celery seed, and pepper. Cook over low heat until bubbly. Remove from heat and stir in water and vinegar. Heat to boiling, stirring constantly. Boil one minute.

Pour mixture over sliced cooled potatoes, add bacon and stir. This dish can be kept warm in a crock-pot until serving.

Cucumber Salad

Sue Broyles
Rapelje, Montana

Sue Broyles got this recipe from an old Home Economists cookbook. It is Sue's favorite cucumber salad recipe because she says she rarely has sour cream on hand.

1-2	tablespoons vinegar, or as desired
1/2	cup buttermilk
1/2	cup Best Foods mayonnaise
4	medium cucumbers, thinly sliced
1	small onion, grated
	salt to taste
	parsley flakes
	paprika

Combine vinegar, buttermilk, and mayonnaise; add cucumbers and onion. Season with salt and parsley flakes and toss lightly. Sprinkle with paprika. (Sour cream may be substituted for buttermilk and mayonnaise.)

6 servings

Galades Salad (A Vegetable Salad)

Sara Johnson
Bozeman, Montana

This recipe came from Sara Johnson's mom via Galade. She says it is much better after 24 hours.

1 medium head fresh cauliflower, chopped

1 1/2 stalks fresh broccoli, chopped

1 cup peas, cooked and drained

1 medium red onion, sliced and left as rings

1 4-ounce jar marinated artichoke hearts, drained and chopped

1 16-ounce can sliced black olives, drained

1 16-ounce package mozzarella cheese, chopped

1 8-ounce bottle Italian salad dressing

salt and pepper, to taste

lettuce

Put all vegetables and cheese in a big bowl, add dressing, and refrigerate overnight. Stir to marinate. Add salt and pepper to taste. Salad can be served over lettuce.

Broccoli Salad

Dorothy Kern
Bozeman, Montana

Dorothy is a favorite Quilting in the Country teacher. After retiring as an elementary school teacher, she found a great love - quilting. Her enthusiasm is contagious.

Salad:

1   large bunch
     broccoli, chopped

1/2 pound bacon, crumbled

1/2 cup salted
     sunflower seeds

1/2 cup currents

1   small onion,
     finely chopped

1   cup fresh mushrooms,
     chopped (optional)

1/2 cup cheese,
     shredded (optional)

     red onion,
     chopped (optional)

     peanuts or
     cashews (optional)

Dressing:

1   cup mayonnaise

2   tablespoons sugar

4   tablespoons vinegar

Mix all salad ingredients. Add dressing. Serve.

Broccoli Delight

Della Berg, "The Plaid Square"
Glasgow, Montana

Salad:

5	cups broccoli, chopped
1/4	cup onions, chopped
8-10	slices of bacon, cooked and crumbled
1	head cauliflower, chopped
1/4	cup carrot, sliced
1/4	cup celery, sliced
1	can water chestnuts, chopped
1	cup sunflower seeds
1/2	cup raisins (optional)

Dressing:

2	tablespoons sugar
3	tablespoons vinegar
1	cup mayonnaise

Mix dressing ingredients well. Stir all salad ingredients together and top with the dressing.

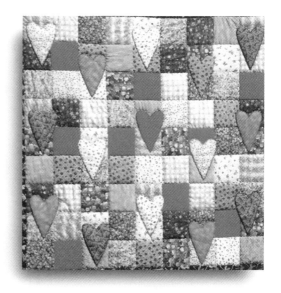

Bacon Broccoli Salad

Patty Weightman
Bozeman, Montana

Salad:

1   large head broccoli, cut into bite-size pieces

5-6   slices bacon, cooked and broken small

1/4   cup sunflower seeds

1/4   cup raisins (use 1/2 cup if preferred)

Dressing:

1/2   cup mayonnaise

1/3   cup water

1   tablespoon barbecue sauce

1 1/2   teaspoons white vinegar

1 1/2   teaspoons dried chives

1/4   teaspoon garlic powder

1/4   teaspoon ground pepper

Combine salad ingredients in a large bowl. In a small mixing bowl, combine dressing ingredients and pour over salad. Mix well and chill for at least 1 hour.

Fresh Broccoli Salad

Eva Veltkamp
Bozeman, Montana

Salad:

4 cups broccoli,
   coarsely chopped

1 red onion,
   finely chopped

1 cup cheddar
   cheese, shredded

10 slices crisp
   bacon, crumbled

Dressing:

1 cup mayonnaise

1/2 cup sugar

4 tablespoons red
   wine vinegar

Toss all salad ingredients.
Mix dressing and pour over
vegetables. Chill.

Guacamole Salad

Jane Quinn
Bozeman, Montana

3 avocados, pureed with
   shells reserved

1/3 cup mayonnaise

1 tablespoon salt

1/2 teaspoon chili powder

3/4 teaspoon garlic powder

   dash Tabasco sauce

2 tablespoons lemon juice

1 medium tomato,
   peeled and chopped

1/3 cup green onions, sliced

1/3 cup celery, sliced

1/2 green pepper, diced

Blend avocado puree with
mayonnaise, seasonings, and
lemon juice. Fold in remaining
ingredients, chill thoroughly. To
serve, pile into avocado shells and
garnish with crisp greens.

Serves 6-8

Carrot Salad - Two Versions

Maria Wolslagel
Bozeman, Montana

Every home has its favorite "house" salad. This is Maria's mom's recipe for carrot salad.

1	pound carrots, grated
3	medium apples, diced
2	sticks celery, finely sliced
1/2	cup seedless raisins
3	level tablespoons mayonnaise
3	level tablespoons Miracle Whip salad dressing
1/2	teaspoon salt

For both versions, combine all ingredients and mix well.

However, this is the version the kids preferred...

1	pound carrots, grated
1/2	cup seedless raisins
1/2	teaspoon salt
	sprinkle of sugar
	enough mayonnaise to moisten

Take good care of your friends because there are times when you won't be any good to anyone-and they'll only love you from habit.
Garrison Keillor

Index

Dressings

Fruit Salads

Grain Salads

Green Salads

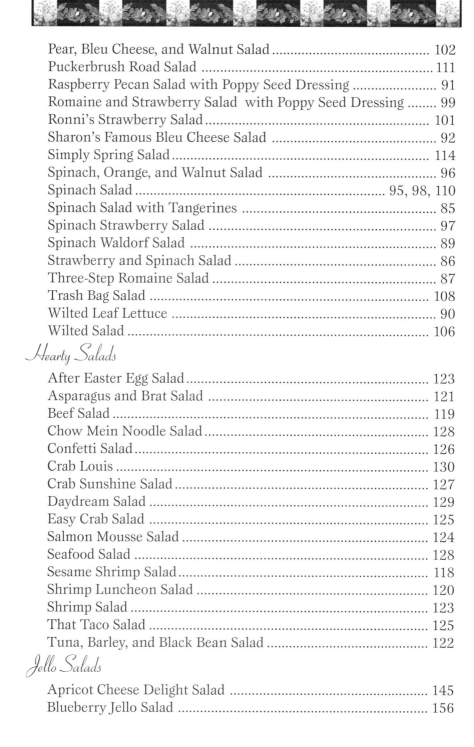

Hearty Salads

Jello Salads

Legume Salads

Pasta Salads

Ramen Salads

Veggie Salads

Notes

Notes

Notes

Notes

Notes

Notes

Notes